SEEKING GOD'S PRESENCE

Barbara Barrow

Trilogy Christian Publishers
A Wholly Owned Subsidiary of Trinity Broadcasting Network
2442 Michelle Drive
Tustin, CA 92780

For information, address Trilogy Christian Publishing
Rights Department, 2442 Michelle Drive, Tustin, Ca 92780.
Trilogy Christian Publishing/ TBN and colophon are trademarks of Trinity Broadcasting Network.

For information about special discounts for bulk purchases, please contact Trilogy Christian Publishing.

Manufactured in the United States of America

10 9 8 7 6 5 4 3 2 1

Library of Congress Cataloging-in-Publication Data is available.

ISBN 978-1-64088-629-2 (Print Book)
ISBN 978-1-64088-630-8 (ebook)

Contents

Preface

Have you at any time encountered something so infinitely shocking, you were left wondering, "How will I ever overcome this?" Perhaps at one time or another you've experienced what felt to be a hurricane screaming, "It's hopeless!"

If your mind answered yes, then welcome to the world of the human soul.

Our soul consists of our mind, our will, and our emotions; and our soul is capable of being a merry-go-round of ups and downs. Yet it is also capable of existing in peace and tranquility. The choice is entirely your decision. Which would you rather own?

> In as much as we refute arguments and theories and reasonings and every proud and lofty thing that sets itself up against the true knowledge of God; and we lead every thought and purpose away captive into the obedience of Christ (the Messiah, the Anointed one). (2 Cor. 10:5, AMP)

Notice that, first of all, we must refute arguments; in other words, we must deny a statement, thought, or any imagination or accusation that would be argumentative to God's word.

The word *accusation* reminds us that Satan is the accuser of the brethren.

> Then I heard a loud voice in heaven say: "Now have come the salvation and the power and the kingdom of our God, and the authority of his Christ. For the accuser of our brothers, who accuses them before our God day and night, has been hurled down. They overcame him by the blood of the Lamb and the word of their testimony; they did not love their lives so much as to shrink from death. (Rev. 12:10–11, NIV)

Satan is the enemy *of* our souls, and the battleground is *in* our souls. He will whisper an idea or thought to set you up for a deceptive "thinking match." If you entertain this game long enough, you will begin to feel dissatisfied or emotionally weary. If allowed to develop, then Satan has a foothold in the doorway of your mind. Because of dissatisfaction, you will begin to complain. When you complain, your spirit becomes overwhelmed.

> I remembered God and was troubled: I complained and my spirit was overwhelmed. (Ps. 77:3, KJV)

> In everything you do stay away from complaining and arguing. (Phil. 2:14, TLB)

Notice the trail that will lead you to the place called "overwhelmed."

This place called "overwhelmed" means "defeat completely," "overpower," "having a strong emotional effect on."

This is not a fun place. It is a place of pure emotional hell.

I don't know about you, but I have felt overwhelmed at times, and once I was there, it was harder to recover than it would have been to simply copy the apostle Paul. His instructions were to cast down those imaginations and thoughts. The thinking match benefited me in no way.

It is so much better to eat the word of God. It is sweet to the taste.

> O taste and see that the LORD is good! Happy is the man who takes refuge in him. (Ps. 34:8, RSV)

> Oh, put God to the test and see how kind he is! See for yourself the way his mercies shower down on all who trust in him. (Ps. 34:8–10, TLB)

Doesn't God's way sound so much better?

Satan can only enter a born-again believer in three areas—the lust of the eyes, the lust of the flesh, or the pride of life (ambition of self). We are the only ones who can grant him entrance through these areas, and we are the ones who are responsible to "*lead* every thought and purpose *away captive.*" Satan's thoughts and purposes are for one thing and one thing only—to kill, steal, or destroy you and God's plan for your life. This is the only reason Satan comes to you (John 10:10).

If Satan can gain entrance through any of these areas, he can temporarily defeat you. If Satan can, he will use every available resource to destroy your life and prevent you from entering the joy of your salvation. But he can only defeat you if you allow him to.

The word *captive* denotes there has to have been a battle of opposing forces. In a battle, someone has to be the captor (a person who confines another), and someone has to be the captive (the one who has been taken prisoner). *We*, the blood-bought overcomers in Christ Jesus, are to take the thoughts that are contrary to the word of God; and *we* are responsible to take *them captive* into the obedience of Christ.

We first cast them down when we refute them. If they are cast down, then leave them there, and don't pick them back up and meditate on them anymore. If you do, you will be back on your way to riding the merry-go-round of emotional ups and downs.

After we cast them down, then we lead them or take them captive. We will not be able to lead them captive unless they are first cast down. If they are still in your thought life, in your mind, they are not doing anything but bringing confusion and dissatisfaction to your soul. They will stay there until *you* take violent action against them.

Remember what we already know that according to Revelation 12:10, Satan was cast down. God didn't waste any time by reasoning with him.

That is the example we have for doing the same thing with his ploys.

By casting down thoughts and imaginations that exalt themselves against the knowledge of God, you are preferring and choosing not to entertain the thought that is bringing chaos or torment to your mind. If there is chaos or tormenting thoughts roaming around in your mind, then your emotions are going to respond accordingly. What does that mean?

You will develop an attitude. Probably you will be in a bad mood. You will become depressed. More than likely, you will cry, or in some cases, people have been known to "self-medicate" their hurting mind. They *will* themselves to proceed down a path of self-destruction of drinking or drugs. All they are trying to accomplish is to obtain some peace of mind.

Satan will come to bring up past mistakes that you have already been forgiven of. Cast them down by using the word of God against the accusation (1 John 1:9).

Satan will come to tempt you with thoughts of "Perhaps the grass is greener on the other side of the fence." You know what I'm talking about.

We used to live on a lake. The road that led to our house was still considered enough in the country so that the owners of this ranch had these cute little donkeys. Nearly every time we passed by them, they would be grazing in this particular field by the road. Usually, one of the donkeys would have his head stretched through the fence as far as his little head would reach. The grass was no different on the other side of that fence, but it just looked better to him. It didn't fill him up any more than the beautiful grass he was standing on. His head would get stuck at times, and he would struggle to get out of the clutch of the fence railing.

It is the same with us. We sometimes act no differently than the little donkey. Pride will cause us to reach out for something that looks better to us or we think will make us look better. The lust of the flesh will want to reach out for something and, after obtaining it, will cause us heartache and misery. Discouragement comes, and defeat has taken its trophy.

There are a number of ways or circumstances that Satan will use to try to trip you into getting over into a weakened state, and if he can succeed, he will take your mind for his prey. Once he has your mind, your body will correspond. Whoever controls your mind controls your body. We must have our minds renewed to the word of God. When this is intact, our bodies remain under control to the Spirit of God.

> For you were bought at a price; therefore glorify God in your body and in your spirit, which are God's. (1Corinthians 6:20, NKJV)

Satan only understands one thing, and that is authority. By submitting yourself to God, you are resisting the devil, and when you resist the devil, he will flee from you (James 4:7).

Then and only then will you be able to enjoy the peace of mind that comes from the knowledge of God.

Search Me

> Search me, Oh God and know my heart. Try me and know my thoughts and see if there be any wicked way in me and lead me in the way everlasting. (Ps. 139:23, KJV)

Have you ever asked God to search your heart?

When you approach God, it is a good time to ask for that wonderful open and honest request. One thing I admire about David is the fact that his heart was honest before God. We have to get honest with God and be open before him. He knows everything you have done, everything you are going to do, and every thought that comes into your mind. You cannot hide anything from God that he doesn't already know. It is a good time to come clean with God as you approach him to worship him. If you are not clean before him, your worship is going to be hindered, and it won't minister to God. If you are not clean before him when you come to him with a request, your prayer will be filtered with doubt and unholiness, and you won't receive your petition.

If you have sin in your life, confess your sin, and let God in! Go ahead and feel free to do business with God. Say to him from your heart, "Get into me and examine me intimately. I want you to be private and personal with me in my innermost being. I am inviting you in. Find out and discern my heart. Take my heart apart piece by piece if you have to, and if you see anything that grieves you or is hurtful, please remove it. Lead and guide me in the right direction. Straighten me out if you must, but please do it. Test me in order to see if I am suitable, effective, or pleasant and see if my thought life, my meditations, and my opinions are pleasing to you. Test me and find the quality of my heart."

David also said, "Let the words of my mouth and the meditation of my heart be acceptable in Your sight, O Lord, my strength and my redeemer" (Ps. 19:14, NKJV).

Like David, we must have our words, our unspoken thoughts, and the plotting of our heart pleasing to God. We give God permission to search us, to intimately examine us, and to bring needed change. But God is not a rapist! It is not his nature to violently seize upon someone and force his way. We must freely give him the search warrant and willingly accept what he finds in us. If there is something that doesn't please God, we must be willing and obedient to make the change that will benefit us, God, and his kingdom.

It is interesting that the word *warrant* originally meant "protector," "safeguard," and "protect from danger" (Oxford

University Press Dictionary). Hallelujah! It is for our own benefit and profit to give God the search warrant, the permission to search us.

God desires to protect us and safeguard us so that we will continue in steadfast faith.

> That the genuineness of your faith, being much more precious than gold that perishes, though it is tested by fire, may be found to praise, honor, and glory at the revelation of Jesus Christ. (1 Pet. 1:7, NKJV)

Gold is one of the most precious and costly metals as such symbolizing the characteristics of God. The value of purified faith can be associated with the value of purified gold. Gold was used in abundance in the most holy place of the tabernacle and the temple, where God revealed himself to the High Priest. Now we are the temple of the Holy Spirit, and we tabernacle God's presence. Shouldn't we willingly and gladly live sanctified, purified, and holy lives?

Be on Guard

> Keep and guard your heart with all vigilance and *above* all that you guard, for out of it flow the springs of life. Put away from you false and dishonest speech and willful and contrary talk put far from you. Let your eyes look right on [with fixed purpose], and let your gaze be straight before you. Consider well the path of your feet, and let all of your ways be established and ordered aright. Turn

not aside to the right hand or to the left;
remove your foot from evil. (Prov. 4:23–
27, AMP)

The KJV says to keep your heart with all diligence. The word *diligence* comes from the Hebrew root word meaning "to hedge about" (as with thorns), i.e., "to guard"; generally "to protect," "to tend to" (Strong's Greek/Hebrew Definitions).

As I was ministering to the Lord early one morning, I was thanking him for ministering to a woman who attends our church. God spoke wonderful encouraging words to her about her son. As he was speaking through the prophet, my heart could feel the emotions she was experiencing. I sensed our hearts were beating in harmony and rhapsody.

As I continued to minister to the Lord, I also reminded him of his promise to me that my heart would be right before him, yet I was wanting his assurance that my heart *was* right and would not be lifted up with pride or arrogance.

The Lord showed me something wonderful although I didn't quite understand what it meant. I wondered if what I was seeing was really from God or if I wanted it so much that I was imagining it.

When are we going to just trust God with all of our heart?

I saw my heart and surrounding it was a hedge of thorns. It looked as though the hedge of thorns was protecting my heart by not allowing anything to enter that was contrary to God. The weight (God's glory) of the hedge was heavy enough to keep pride or arrogance from rising within me. Then the Holy Spirit reminded me of Proverbs 4:23 to keep my heart with all diligence. How humbled I felt when I read about the meaning of the word *diligence*. God had showed me that my heart was already hedged about with a protection of thorns!

All I could do was worship him even more intensely.

> Then came Jesus forth wearing the crown
> of thorns and the purple robe. And Pilate
> saith unto them, "Behold the man."
> (John 19:54, KJV)

Then came Jesus forth. What is coming forth out of you? Is Jesus coming forth? Jesus wore a crown of thorns on his head, and he wore a purple robe on his body.

Jesus places a thorny hedge around the crown of our heart, signifying his sovereignty. He is to have the supreme power and authority over the issues of life that flow out of us.

Jesus came forth, wearing the purple robe, representing the burden of the world's sin and judgment that he was to bear.

Jesus wore a burden for the world. It was, by analogy, constant accompaniment (Strong's Greek/Hebrew Definitions). Jesus instructs *us*, though, to come unto him if we are burdened down with anything, and he will give us rest (Matt. 11:28). Instead of having a constant burden wearing on us, Jesus wants to *accompany* us through the person of the Holy Spirit and fill up and fulfill our souls and give us rest.

The implication of the *hedge* around our heart is the same Hebrew word that is mentioned in Psalm 91:11: "For he shall give his angels charge over thee, to "keep" thee in all thy ways" (KJV).

God will *keep* us in all our ways by protecting us, by hedging about us as with thorns. When we are kept in *all our ways*, we will be kept in the walk that God has specified for each one of us. Each one of us has been summoned and gifted with an anointing to accomplish our call in life. The Holy Spirit will accompany us and lead us so that we will reach the finished goal, the purpose for our life, our destiny.

If you haven't already asked God for that *hedge as of thorns* to be around your heart, to guard it, why don't you ask him right now?

> As the deer pants for the water brooks, So pants my soul for you, O God. My soul thirsts for God, for the living God. When shall I come and appear before God? (Ps. 42:1–2, NKJV)

Have you ever been so thirsty that you would do anything for a drink of cool, refreshing, life-sustaining water?

Notice the analogy in verse one between the natural and the spiritual. The deer is so drained and thirsty that it is panting, desperately seeking to find some satisfying water. Have you ever seen an animal that is panting? It is breathing with short quick breaths. It is usually the result of exertion or even excitement, maybe from running for a long period of time without resting. Maybe it is from the excitement it experiences when it finds its way out of a dangerous trap. But this passage implies that the deer pants because it is thirsty for a drink of water from the brook. Have you ever been so thirsty that you panted for water, and you thought you would die if you didn't get a drink of water?

The author of this Psalm is so beautifully describing his thirst for the Spirit of God—his thirst for God is as intense as a deer panting for water from a stream. The deer is panting to drink from the stream of water, and in the same sense, this writer is longing to drink from the fountain of God; he is just as thirsty as the deer that has been running and out of breath. The only thing it is desiring is something to quench its thirst. It must find the brook. We must find the living fountain.

I believe the reason people aren't thirsty for God is that they feel satisfied where they are in God. They don't feel thirsty. If they did, they would certainly drink more from the water brook. Some meanings for the word *brook* are "channel" and "strong piece."

The deer *longs* for the brook. The deer is looking for that channel of water so that when it gathers there, the thirst will be satisfied or taken away, and its dry, thirsty body will be restored. It craves this. And so our soul, the seat of our emotions and passions, must be trained to thirst or crave God, our strong piece! Only his presence can satisfy, refresh, and recover our weary souls. The word *God* in verse one of this scripture means "the works or special possessions of God." Then the writer adds "the living God," meaning "revival and renewal." Isn't that interesting? We are to crave the special possessions of God and the revival and renewal of God!

> Every scripture is God breathed [given by his inspiration] and profitable for instruction, for reproof and conviction of sin, for correction of error and discipline to obedience, [and] for training in righteousness [holy living, in conformity to God's will in thought, purpose and action] so that the man of God may be complete and proficient, well fitted and thoroughly equipped for every good work." (2 Tim. 3:16–17 AMP)

According to Timothy, we will profit, gain and advance if we receive and apply to our minds the word of God. And because it would benefit us to behave in accordance with those words, let's determine in our hearts, before we go any further, that we will apply these God-inspired words to our life.

"Where can I go and meet with God?"

"Where can I go and give attention to observe God?"

I am so glad you asked.

> Seek the Lord and his strength; Yearn for and seek his face and To be in his presence continually. (1 Chron. 16:11, AMP)

Desiring God

Have you ever felt so lacking for something on the inside of you and you just didn't know what it was or what to do about it? In the natural, maybe all is well or maybe not, maybe your needs are being met, maybe not. But there is just something you are desiring and nothing that you do, nothing that you buy seems to satisfy that need. Maybe you are not interested in the things of God enough to get involved with volunteering at church. Maybe you have trouble making it to church on a regular basis, and when you get there, it seems as though you have wasted your time. You are not really interested in the sermon... After all, it doesn't apply to you.

Maybe it is because you are dry and barren on the inside. Sometimes we can be so dry that we don't even know we are dry until we are wet!

People have run from church to church waiting for *something* to satisfy them, to satisfy their thirst and hunger—waiting for *something* to give them some joy, some peace. Is it that our spirit is dead? Is it that we haven't heard enough word preached for the last twenty years? What is it then? Do we need to get born again, again?

If we have been born again, then our spirit man is already new.

Second Corinthians 5:17 reads, "Therefore if any person is [ingrafted] in Christ (the Messiah) he is a new creation (a new creature altogether); the old [previous moral and spiritual condition] has passed away. Behold the fresh and new has come" (AMP).

All your spirit man will ever want to do is thirst and crave God, for he is fashioned after God. So it is in the realm of your soul, your mind, your will, and your emotions that need to be refreshed and trained to desire the special possessions of God and trained to give attention to and learn about God.

My soul, my mind, and my desires must *learn or be trained* to thirst for God, for the special possessions of God, and for the life-giving, reviving renewal of God.

But how can our minds be made to desire such things? How in the world can we find time to shut our minds off long enough to train our minds to seek after spiritual things?

Our minds are busy all day long dealing with cares, being involved in trials and situations that literally pull us down and seemingly leave a weight on us. So what do we do? One of the ways to get refreshed in our thinking is to have our minds renewed to God's word. Since his words are life unto them who find them and health to all their flesh (Prov. 4:22), it would be wisdom then to learn and practice the words and teachings of the one who made the world that we are living in that constantly pulls on us. How thoughtful and wonderful of God to provide us with "survival skills" or overcoming truths through his word.

We are to renew our minds through the word: "And be not conformed to this world, but be ye transformed by the renewing of your mind" (Rom. 12:2, KJV). Since faith comes by hearing and hearing by the Word of God (Rom. 10:17, NKJV), hearing the word over and over and over and over until it sinks down into your spirit is one way to renew your mind.

Just listen to some of the songs that the young people (not all of them, praise God) of today are listening to, and your mind will feel like it is going nuts since all songs don't edify, comfort, or lift you. What you are hearing is not building your faith in God which is from where your strength has to come. In the midst of a life-threatening situation or some other test, certain music will not minister to your soul. Only God-breathed, God-anointed music will lift, encourage, and bring the comfort needed for a hopeful victory. Only God's words can bring life. Since faith comes by hearing and hearing, your faith might become built up in things other than the word of God.

Whatever is on the inside of you will eventually come out. If you hear evil or negative reports long enough, you will eventually begin to speak those reports or words. Out of the abundance or overflow of the heart, the mouth will speak (Luke 6:4, AMP). It is of great reward to set a guard over your words. David asked that the words of his mouth and the meditation of his heart be acceptable in God's sight (Ps. 19:14, NKJV). I believe that should be included in our daily prayers to God.

In Proverbs 4:23, God warns us to keep our heart with all diligence. The Living Bible Translation reads, "Above all else guard your affections. For they influence everything else in your life." Your affections, whether good or bad, will definitely have an influence on your mind. Therefore, I ask the question, "What do you want to be influencing *your* mind?"

Matthew 16:23 says we should have in our minds the things of God. Jesus had been explaining to his disciples how he would suffer many things, be killed, and be raised the third day. But Peter, in all good conscience, tried to explain to Jesus that he had it all wrong. After all, Jesus was God, and how could such a thing happen to God?

Jesus rebuked Peter and told him that because he was not mindful of the things of God (because of the lack of understanding and because he did not have his mind set upon the things of God), he was an offense or a stumbling block to him.

What a sad thing to hear someday that we were a stumbling block or offense because of what our minds had been set upon or not been set upon.

> Let this mind be in you which was also in Christ Jesus. (Phil 2:5, NKJV)

> Let this same attitude and purpose and [humble] mind be in you which was in Christ Jesus: [Let him be your example in humility]. (AMP)

Matthew 22:37 says Jesus said to love the Lord our God with all of our heart, all of our strength, and all of our *mind* (the implication of exercising your mind through deep thought, to get understanding) (Strong's Greek/Hebrew Definitions).

Luke 21:14 says Jesus told his disciples to make up their *minds* not to worry about what to say… He would give them word to say when they witnessed.

Not only should we have our minds renewed, but it is our responsibility to be determined to keep our minds on God's law and our ears tuned to the Holy Spirit.

Psalm 119:165 encourages us, "Those who love Your laws have great peace of heart and mind and do not stumble" (TLB).

Don't you love that? I believe it is very important and reassuring to know that we can have strong peace in our minds when we set our affections toward God's instructions for our lives. When we have our affections set on God's instructions or law, our focus will be on *him*, making it impossible for us to stumble. Offenses will *come* to us, but if we love God's teachings and actually try to live by them, we will not have a desire to strike back at the *offender*. Instead, we will feel compassion and pray for them. That is when we can say that we are walking in love.

The apostle Paul exhorts us in Philippians 4:4 (NKJV), "To rejoice (to be 'cheerful' i.e., calmly happy) in the Lord always (at all times) and again to rejoice" (Strong's Greek/Hebrew Definitions).

In verses 6 through 8, we are commanded to "Be anxious for nothing, but in everything by prayer and supplication, with thanksgiving, let your request be made known to God, and the peace of God, which surpasses all understanding, will guard your hearts and *minds* through Christ Jesus."

Please understand this.

Spending time *in* God's Word and getting understanding and spending time *with* him is the key to peace. Paul exhorts us in verse 8, "Whatever is true, whatever is worthy of reverence *and* honorable *and* seemly, whatever is just, whatever is lovely *and* lovable, whatever is kind *and* winsome *and* gracious, if there is any virtue *and* excellence, if there is anything worthy of praise, think on *and* weigh *and* take account of these things [*fix your minds on them*]" (AMP). That's a full-time job in itself!

I don't know about you, but it sounds to me as if there are enough things to think about to keep our minds at peace and our moods elevated so that we are not in a "bad mood" all of the time. There are enough things to think upon that will refresh our minds so that we will not react in an unholy way when an unpleasant situation is presented to us. Have you ever noticed how often unpleasant situations present themselves to you? I have felt before, at the end of the day, that all I want to do is just go to bed and pull the covers over my head and hide out for a while. "Take the phone off the hook, Jim, and order pizza."

We all have felt like that at one time or another, and if you never have felt overwhelmed, you are blessed! Pray for the rest of us! I hope you never will have to experience any stress, but if you do, just realize that's life! Stress is everywhere. It is impossible to be in this world and have everything go your way. That is fantasy land. But when we turn everything over to Jesus and tell him that we can't handle everything and we need his help, he'll give us strength to overcome every obstacle. We will still have to go through things, but we will go through and make it to the other side in victory!

We may get down, but we can't stay down. That is why it is called the Good News! God's Word, which has been deposited on the inside of us, will always come back to us and provide *overcoming* faith and hope for a better tomorrow. God promises us that our path will only grow brighter and brighter (Prov. 4:18). There is the possibility, though, that you might not have *enough* of the overcoming faith. It is the word of God that feeds our spirit man. Maybe your spirit man is starving because you haven't been feeding on the word of God. Could he look malnourished? There is the possibility that you have just not had the desire to *want* to hear the Word of God.

Maybe you have heard the Word and know what to do, but you lack the *strength* to enforce it. Your mind seems to be running in a hundred different directions. You don't have time to stop and spend time with the Lord in order to hear him. You want to, but you just don't have the time. Someone once told me that you will find the time to do what you really want to or have to do, and I have found that to be the truth in most cases. It may have to be late at night; but whatever it takes, I encourage you to read the word of God, ask God to give you understanding of it, and allow it to settle into your spirit man.

I personally believe that early in the morning while your mind is still clear is the best time to get still before the Lord and listen to him. Listen to what he is wanting to say to you about your day. After all, doesn't he smooth and straighten out the road ahead of you? Don't you want to know where those places are so that you can walk in uprightness and avoid pitfalls? If you don't have a desire for the things of God, won't you simply ask him to give you a desire for him?

Not only is it important to spend time *in* the Word, but it is necessary to find some time during the day to spend *with* the Lord…just you and him. Get alone before the Lord, and stay long enough for your mind to become quiet so it will be able to receive his thoughts. God will show you he is God if we will get still before him (Ps. 46:10).

If we allow God's renewal of strength and power to rule in us, our mind will be *subject to and controlled by* our spirit man (through the Holy Spirit), and our actions will correspond. Therefore we will walk in the ways of righteousness and peace.

One thing have I asked of the Lord, that I will seek, inquire for, *and* [insistently] require: that I may dwell in the house of the Lord [in his presence] all the days of my life, to behold and gaze upon the beauty [the sweet attractiveness and the delightful loveliness] of the Lord and to meditate, consider, *and* inquire in his temple. (Ps. 27:4, AMP)

2

Take a Drink

The deer that pants for the water is a deer that is craving or crying out for the one thing that will sustain its life. It is crying out for the only thing that will satisfy and keep it strong. It is requiring a drink of water.

Deer have keen survival skills. One of the survival skills it well knows is that it *requires* water. It will risk everything. It will risk its life to get some refreshing, life-sustaining water. It *must* have it to survive. It could lose its life because in order to get to the brook, it may have to get out into the open and expose itself to danger. It is risky, but nothing else will satisfy the deer's thirst, so it will take a chance on losing its life.

In the same context, it's risky to your pride (who wants any of that?) to humble yourself and allow God to have his way in you. There is the possibility that something unpleasant might happen! There might actually be something in you that God doesn't like! Could it be possible that God wants you to be pure in your thoughts and actions? When you begin "drinking of the living water" of God or the new wine as it is referred to, you won't care what anyone thinks. All you will want is *more* of God's presence and his character. You will begin to learn of him and become so thirsty that you will actually *crave* his presence. You will *ask* him to change you because you will fall so in love with Jesus! Because you're in love with him, place your trust in him, knowing he will not remove or add anything to your life that will not be beneficial and helpful to you. You may be asking the question, "How do I get to that place in God?"

That comes from drinking and drinking and drinking the living water which is the Holy Spirit that comes from God! That place in God comes when you have made a habit of drinking in the Spirit of God. We need to be full of it. What are you full of?

Are you full of pride? Bitterness? Envy? Jealousy? Strife? Anger? Discontentment? Are you sad all of the time? Are you controlled by your flesh? Are you moody?

Jesus said, "If anyone is thirsty, let him come to me and drink" (John 7:37, NIV). You must come to Jesus for it. If you don't have a strong desire for the Holy Spirit, simply ask him to make you thirsty. Ask him to give you a desire for the things of God, and then come to him by faith and drink. Don't try to pray while you are drinking. It doesn't work. I've tried it. This is a time with God where you are *receiving* only. It is not a time to give of yourself through prayer. Simply ask the Holy Spirit to give the presence of God to you. Place yourself in a relaxing position and believe you are *drinking in* the Spirit of God. But how?

> Jesus told the woman at the well, "Whoever drinks of the water that I shall give him will never thirst." (John 4:14, NKJV)

I believe this scripture is implying we must come before the Lord and drink of the Spirit of God and *absorb* his Spirit (his living water) like a sponge. According to the *Strong's* Greek/Hebrew Definition, the word *drink* in this verse means to "imbibe." I found it very interesting that two of the definitions of the word *imbibe*, according to Oxford University Press Dictionary, are "humorous drink" and "to *absorb*" (ideas or knowledge). As you drink, God will give you ideas, and you will become more familiar with God.

What does a sponge do? One thing it does is *absorb* water! Not only must we absorb the living water (Holy Spirit) of God, we must learn to do it on a continual basis. Become a habitual drinker of the Spirit of God, continually receiving the renewal of God's strength and power! It will become in us a source of power and a source of peace and refreshment. By doing so, we will move to a higher place of position in God, and it will satisfy the needs and desire of the soul. We won't be led by our feelings but rather live in a constant state of pleasure and peace.

It is amusing to me that a definition of the word *imbibe* is "to take in a humorous drink." No wonder people get *under the influence* of God and begin laughing. It really happens this way. It really will give you everything you just read. The key, though, is humbling yourself before God and admitting to him that you *need* his presence, you are *thirsty, and to ask him to give you more of him.* God is so willing to give to you what you ask of him. In fact, he is more willing to give of himself *to* you than you are to ask *for* him.

Once you ever feel his presence come upon you, you will become addicted to him. You will always want *more.* That is why you might hear someone crying out to God, "Give me more, Lord!" He is so satisfying, and all you want to do is stay in his presence. Isn't it wonderful to know that there is something we can become addicted to that will actually benefit us?

We once gathered together on Tuesday nights at my church solely for the purpose to receive "more of God's presence." Out of his presence comes his righteousness, peace, and joy in the Holy Spirit.

We met corporately at the church. If you decide to have a group "soaking," be sure you are meeting in a safe place where there is nothing to distract you or interrupt what the Holy Spirit is doing. It is all right to bring children. After all, they need to be exposed to this atmosphere as often as possible.

There were a couple of women who brought their children, but they would lie down and receive God's presence, or maybe they would sit in the back of the church and do their homework. Still, they were old enough to know to respect the atmosphere that the Holy Spirit had created in which he wanted to move.

Make certain there is adequate room for individuals to lie down if they want to. There is something about posturing to receive. I believe it is symbolic of the intimacy of receiving impartation from the Holy Spirit. If you feel more comfortable in a sitting position, that's okay too. The main thing is to get comfortable so that you can relax and get ready to "get lost in God." I have literally felt like I didn't know where I was for a moment when I got up to leave the building. It's because you become so saturated in him and so focused on him that you are unaware of what's going on around you. So if you stay that focused on God long enough, that is when you will feel "drunk" or "lost in God."

It is good to dim the lights, because it allows you to feel more relaxed. Don't have the lights so dim that you might trip over someone! That is another reason it needs to be a safe place a place where people don't have to be concerned about *anything*. Let them know that when they enter the designated place of "soaking" that they are entering a place of rest—a place to meet and get loved on by God. Assure them that God wants to love them and does not want to beat them up because they have been bad. It's God's goodness not his punishment that leads men to repentance (Rom. 2:4).

Also have soft anointed music playing. The Holy Spirit is drawn to the worship music.

It is the time in which you are "under the influence" that you will feel God's tender love for you. In return, you cannot help but fall absolutely more in love with Jesus.

As I mentioned earlier, we met together at my church on Tuesday nights from about 7:00 p.m. to 8:30 p.m. We gathered there corporately to bask in God's presence—to become more like him.

There is something wonderful about a corporate anointing, but it is not necessary to meet corporately to receive. You can receive God's presence while you are alone at home, driving in your car, buying groceries, or mowing the yard. But it is best to get alone with God in a private place so that you can focus and give him your undivided attention. That way, you are not only receiving his presence; you are free from distractions so that you can clearly hear his voice.

Allow me to explain the purpose of the Tuesday night soaking meetings and what happens:

1. It is to drink. Jesus said *if* anyone was thirsty that they should come to him and drink (John 7:37). There seems to be a greater anointing when you come together with other people for the same purpose. Although there may be twenty people gathered together at the same place for soaking, you

can still get alone with Jesus and soak and listen. People bring their pillows, some bring a blanket, and they find somewhere on a comfortable pew and lie down and begin. Some go to sleep, but that is okay. God has done some of his most beautiful work while man was asleep. Look what happened to Adam while he was sleeping! While you are sleeping, God can perform "spiritual surgery" and literally remove something that is not needed in you. When you have purposed this time for God and have asked him to speak to you, even though you fall asleep (sometimes, depending upon your day it is impossible to stay awake!), God will still impart unto you exactly what your heart is opened for. You can receive God's presence alone during the day or during the night. Just ask him for it, open your heart to him, and wait.

2. It is to imbibe. Go ahead and have fun… Pretend you are a sponge absorbing God. God will give you ideas and knowledge. Colossians 1:9 tells us that it is possible "to be *filled* with the *knowledge of his will* in all wisdom and spiritual understanding so that we may walk worthy of the Lord, *fully* pleasing him, being fruitful in every good work and *increasing* in the knowledge of God *strengthened* with all might" (NKJV).

3. It is to absorb. *Take in* the presence, the Spirit of God, like a sponge. Sometimes, according to how dry you might be, it might take a while for you to "become fully absorbed." Think about a dry sponge—a really dried-out sponge. It almost looks twisted or warped. If you were to pour water on it, it wouldn't just immediately be softened and full of

water ready for use. No, if you began pouring water on it, what would happen? First of all, it wouldn't receive anything. The water would splash off. But keep pouring long enough, and what would happen then? The sponge would look like it was relaxing, so to speak. It would look like it was softening. Next, you would begin to see it absorbing some of the water. If it remained under the water long enough, you would finally see a sponge that looked and acted like a sponge. It would become useful not only to itself but for another sponge's use! Water would be "oozing" out of the sponge because it had absorbed so much. That is the way God wants us to be: he wants us to be so full of him that *he* is oozing out of us and spilling onto someone else. Sometimes, we don't realize how dry we are until we become wet!

4. It is to take a humorous drink. We drink all we can! When we are in God's presence, he promises to fill us with joy (Ps. 16:11). So the longer we are in his presence, the more joy we are going to experience. We don't pray while we are soaking. Soaking is a time to receive from God. When we pray, we are giving out. We want to use this time to just "take in." If you were drinking water, could you pray at the same time? No. I have tried it. It doesn't work. Again, all "drinking" is about is just coming before the Lord to receive his presence, drinking and absorbing as much of him as we can.

5. It is to hear from God. Ask God to speak to you concerning something that is of importance to you or your family, etc. God is interested in your personal life. He will speak to your mind and give

direction to you. It is possible while waiting in his presence that you will be inspired to do something or say something, either then or maybe for a later time. Even though it could seem silly at the time, remember God's ways are not like our ways, nor his thoughts our thoughts (Isa. 55:8). It could be that God is ridding you of some inhibition that has held you back from moving forward in God. It is so important to simply allow God to be God and do whatever he wants to do. After all, you have come there wanting what God has. Don't worry about what it looks like or what people are thinking. First of all, they are all "drunk" or "under the influence" and don't care anyway. Second of all, there should be someone in leadership there to gently lead you in another direction if it is not of God.

6. It is to have our minds and emotions refreshed. It may take a while for your mind to shut down from your busy day's agenda, usually around ten minutes or so, but please determine to "turn off your mind." The longer you have been a "soaker," the easier it is to turn off your mind. Stop thinking about the day you have just had at work or the hectic day at home or the business that is weighing on your mind. Now this takes training. Even though you *can* "turn off" your mind, if you are not diligent to watch for it, all of the thoughts of the day will try to creep back into your mind. Before long even without realizing it, you are again thinking about that business job, the kids that are giving you trouble or whatever else that has plagued your mind during the day. Eventually, it will dawn on you, "Hey, what am I doing?" And then you can guide

your mind back into the place of peace, thinking on Jesus or the words of the music that are playing. It is a training process. Actually, the Holy Spirit is the one who reminds you to draw your mind back toward him.

7. It is to receive strength for our minds and our physical bodies. I don't know how many times I, like others, have come to the River Soaking wishing that I was at home in my pajamas with my face washed and watching some television so I could wind down for the day. Especially those days when I was awake at 4:30 a.m., studying before I went to work and then straight to the Soaking Service, knowing that I won't get home till after 9:00 p.m. Jesus never said it would be easy. But I have never left the service disappointed, and I have always left relaxed and happier than when I came. So has everyone else that comes. On one occasion, a dear woman told me the following night at church how I healed her leg during the Soaking Service, and she hasn't had any trouble since. I didn't heal her. I only helped her to lie down and told her to let the Lord minister to her. It was the Holy Spirit that brought the healing to her.

8. It is to get before God, to wait on God, to open our hearts up to God and be willing to allow the Holy Spirit to perform "spiritual surgery" on our "internal injuries" that have occurred. "Internal injuries" can occur as a result of our own doings or as a result of something unpleasant incurred by someone else. Sometimes people can be so hurtful to others. They can inflict someone with words that can actually wound a person's heart and tar-

nish their soul. Sometimes, the only way they can be healed is by allowing God to perform spiritual surgery on them. I have found that the injuries most often occurring are those that we inflict upon ourselves. We can get so busy that we are burdened down to the point that we become stressed, and it is all because we can't say no to people. We minister to the point that we are overwhelmed; we become confused, frustrated, and physically tired and mentally stressed. I am not telling you to be neglectful of other's needs and burdens or to be lazy in your church or workplace. Every one of us has a place and service in this world to make it a better place (Gal. 3:18), and we need to contribute our time and energy, but there has to be a balance in every area of our lives. If we allow our minds to become so cluttered and distracted from God, sometimes, even the slightest thing spoken to us will be taken the wrong way, and we will get our feelings hurt. We must train ourselves to listen to what God is saying to us and keep an attitude of prayer. If you get offended by someone, don't stay offended. Be quick to ask God to help you to forgive that person. Ask the Holy Spirit to strengthen you. We need his strength every day. Even Jesus would often get alone to pray. He would go up on a mountain, apart from the crowd. He had to be alone. And when he was alone, he would pray and seek God. He had to because when he came down from that mountain, people immediately began pulling on the anointing. Not only was he God, but he was a man. And although the Spirit of God was upon him without measure or limit (John 3:34, TLB), he still would not do anything unless he first saw the Father do it (John 5:19). He sought God often. He communicated with God often. How often do we seek God? How much do we communicate with God?

9. It is to get into the presence of God. When you are in his presence, there is a feeling of great pleasure and happiness. There is also rejoicing, there is gladness, and there can be glorious times of weeping. I call them glorious times because when I am weeping before the Lord, I am doing so because I feel such a tremendous love for him, and afterward, I am left with such peace and refreshment. I like to be happy and in a good mood, don't you? I don't always feel happy, and I'm not always in a good mood. But thank God I have come to the place that if I recognize I am not in a good mood, I will rebuke it and ask God to forgive me for my "ungodly attitude" as I call it. If I don't recognize it right off, Jim will be happy to help me get into a better mood. For those of you who are married, aren't you thankful for a mate who will help you when you're down?

Having the joy of the Lord is not laughing all of the time; it is simply experiencing a state of gladness. It would be fun to laugh all of the time, although I knew a woman who laughed after everything she said, and it annoyed me. There was nothing wrong with laughing; it just got on my nerves after a while.

We need more laughter because the world we live in is in such dire need of joy. Of course, you are going to laugh when you are glad or happy. But I have been glad, and I have been happy, and I didn't laugh at all. Go ahead and laugh! It will do you good. All I am trying to say to you is don't feel bad if you don't laugh. It took me ten years before I ever started laughing in the Spirit. Ten years.

There is no *law* saying you *must* laugh or have any other manifestations that occur when *under the influence* of the Holy Spirit. But when you do get loose enough, so to speak, and drunk enough from drinking of the new wine, you will find yourself doing things that you didn't think you would ever do. However, whatever you do will be within the guidelines of the Holy Spirit. He will never influence you to do something that will bring harm or embarrassment to the kingdom of God.

The reason laughter is so common to hear is that we become so relaxed in the presence of God. We forget about our problems, and we lose our inhibitions. By that I mean that if you are usually a shy withdrawn person as you receive God's presence long enough, you will slowly become a different person. You will begin to see a boldness that you never had before. You will notice that you are not as withdrawn as you once were.

There was a woman who started coming to our Soaking Service. When she first started coming, she was withdrawn and hardly ever spoke to anyone. She has been coming for about a year now, and you wouldn't recognize her. She has been transformed! She doesn't stay away from others but rather joins some of us on the floor and *parties*.

Earlier, I mentioned that it took me ten years to laugh in the Spirit, and the reason was that I was extremely inhibited. I had been that way all of my life, and I hated it. I hated the fact that I was so shy and timid. God had his work cut out for him, and he was faithful to help me overcome the way I was. Depending upon what the Holy Spirit desires to impart to us (he always knows what we are needing), we sometimes laugh so hard that we can hardly talk or communicate to someone beside us about what the Lord is conveying to us (you don't have to tell anyone what the Lord is saying to you, but if it will minister to someone, go ahead and say it). Sometimes, we just lie down in his presence and let him minister peace and rest to us.

We never know what to expect from the Holy Spirit. Sometimes, I will feel an unction from the Holy Spirit to pray and ask God for a specific direction for the Holy Spirit to flow in. I will then share what he is desiring to do that night corporately for the church. As I lay hands on people and release the Holy Spirit's anointing, he pours out that specific desire on the people, and his will and purpose for the Church is accomplished by their willingness to open up their hearts. (Since I was the leader and the one in charge of these meetings, I had the authority to release God's Spirit as he willed.)

The Holy Spirit is not a rapist—didn't rape Mary. She simply believed in her heart what the messenger angel told her would happen. She was *willing* to receive him. It is the same way with us. If you are willing, he will overshadow you and impart into your spirit a holy desire for a specific purpose and plan of God for the Church, community, or world. You will feel a greater love for Jesus that you hadn't had before.

10. It is to receive God's outpouring of his love so that we will be able to love him. We love God because he first loved us (1 John 4:19).

How can we love others if we don't first love God? We cannot love ourselves if we don't first receive his love. So we surrender and submit our spirit, soul, and our bodies before the Lord and ask his loving Holy Spirit to "*keep coming to us...give us more.*"

In John 4, we find a woman who didn't even know or didn't recognize that she was in the presence of Jesus. But when Jesus told her that the water he would give—and to whoever drinks of it would cause them never to thirst—something stirred within her, and she was interested in what Jesus had to say. She wanted some of that living water. If she would never have to come to that well again and never thirst again, hey, she wanted some! Of course, she didn't know that Jesus was actually speaking life into her as they continued their conversation.

But Jesus told her, "If you knew the gift of God and who it is who says to you, 'Give me a drink' you would have asked him and he would have given you living water" (John 4:10, NKJV).

As the woman remained in his presence, life was imparted to her. Truth about her life was revealed, and her sin was exposed to her. Jesus didn't condemn her; he lovingly pointed out to her that her lifestyle was not what it should be.

Remaining in the presence of God for a period of time will sometimes cause you to feel like an onion! God will lovingly and gently begin peeling off layers of things that aren't exactly holy or pleasing to him. It might hurt at first, but when you begin seeing the beauty of Christ that resides within the midst of you that has been hidden, you will say, "*More, Lord.*"

As the result of being with Jesus for a while, something about the woman at the well was changed, even though she left and went "her way" into the city to the men. Her lifestyle hadn't changed yet, but notice what happens. She went to the men and told them about Jesus, who had told her all things that she had ever done. I am sure that took a while!

The men went out of the city and came to Jesus. This woman had already witnessed enough to cause men to come to the Lord. The Bible says that many of the Samaritans of that city believed in him because of the word of the woman who testified, "He told me all that I ever did" (author's translation). People will recognize you have been with Jesus because you will become bold to witness (Acts 4:13).

They asked Jesus to stay with them, and he did—for two days. And many more believed because of his own word. Then they said to the woman, "Now we believe, not because of what you said, for we ourselves have heard Him and we know that this is indeed the Christ, the Savior of the world" (John 4:41–42, NKJV).

People will listen to you when you tell them about how wonderful the presence of God is, and they might even come to your soaking meeting to get some of God because you told them how wonderful he is. But once they ever "know for themselves" or experience God's presence for themselves, they will never be the same. Many of the Samaritans believed because of the woman's word that Jesus had spoken and they came to see Jesus. It was after being with him for two days that the Samaritans then believed for themselves. They had experienced God for themselves and gained knowledge after they had spent some time in his presence.

> Seek, inquire of and for the Lord, and crave him and his strength (His might and inflexibility to temptation); Seek and require his face and his presence continually evermore. (Ps. 105:4, AMP)

3

Spirit versus Flesh

You can withdraw from the outside world and make all kinds of excuses or reasons, and probably they are good reasons, but there is coming an appointed time by God when you will be required to come back out and get back into the ministry that God has ordained and called you.

Jesus withdrew into a deserted place when he heard about the death of his cousin, John, who had been beheaded by King Herod; he most definitely had reason to withdraw. It was a time of mourning over the death and loss of a loved one, as well as the loss of a great prophet. I believe Jesus was mourning just as much over the fact that the world would not receive light and truth as he was over the fact that his cousin had just been killed.

But Jesus, after mourning, did go out, and when he did, he saw a multitude, and he was moved with compassion.

Whenever you go out and not until you go out, God will show you, and your eyes will be opened to needs. And when God moves you with compassion for them, he will enable you to heal and help them.

All through Jesus's ministry, he was moved with compassion and healed them. But he was always out among the needs in order to see the needs and meet the needs. You don't have to go looking for needs. They will come to you. Problems will just show up. You just have to be in the position to be able to handle them when they present themselves.

I don't even like the sound of the word *need*. When you look in the dictionary under the word *need*, is your picture there?

We are all needy people at one time or other, but God is saying, "There is always going to be a way, and I will supply your every need not according to your riches but according to my riches which are in Christ Jesus."

Where are you positioned?

Jesus Christ is the rock of our salvation. The Bible says we are seated together in heavenly places with Christ Jesus. Aren't you glad we are with Christ Jesus? If we are with Christ Jesus, then we have access to all things pertaining to life and godliness.

Let's look at how Jesus demonstrated this to the disciples.

All things mean all things, doesn't it?

All things that pertain to life and godliness.

In Matthew 14:14, we find a real-life situation—what looks to be a crisis or possible life-threatening situation. The possible ten thousand people (five thousand men, women, and children) had just been with Jesus witnessing healing miracles. They were all pumped, maybe on the verge of trying to get closer to Jesus to discuss their prophecies and talk about their relatives' needs.

Look at this conversation between the natural thinking and the supernatural thinking.

Look at verse 15, and notice what the disciples say to Jesus, and notice what Jesus says to the disciples.

The disciples said (this is the natural man thinking... the logical voice of reasoning),

1) "This is a deserted place (true). Have you ever been in what seems to be a deserted place with no one to help?"
2) "It is late (true). Have you ever been in a late hour and needed God to do something quickly?"
3) "Send the multitude away that they may go into the villages," and
4) "Buy themselves food (sounds logical). Try to do it on your own."

Have you ever told God how and what he should do about something? Maybe God has forgotten or missed something.

Notice Jesus's response; he is thinking in the supernatural realm:

1) "They do not need to go away."

God doesn't respond to us just because we have a need.

When God spoke of his plan of redemption (Gen. 15), it was a response to his own word.

Ephesians 1:11 says, "Who works all things according to the counsel of his will" (NKJV), which is his word. The Word says that Jesus is the Lamb slain before the foundation of the world. It wasn't some kind of plan God had to come up with on the spot. God knows the end from the beginning. He knows it and calls it, and so should we.

2) You give them something to eat.

Can't you just hear the disciples' minds doing flip-flops? They were thinking something like, "We have here within our ability only five loaves of bread and two fish" (I've been to Israel, and the Sea of Galilee does not have any orcas in it, only smaller fish). Those two fish were not, in their minds, going to feed all of those people. (When I go to a restaurant. I can eat more than two fish...can you?) The two fish would have to feed more than five thousand people.

Now all of this was going through their minds. They were tired from the day, and now they were going to have to come up with more fish and bread. What would you have said to Jesus? Little did they realize that not only two fish and five loaves were there, but because Jesus was there, they would have more than enough.

God will never leave you with a need without supplying it. Is Jesus with you? Then you, too, will have more than enough.

Your mind, which is your voice of reasoning, will always kick in and begin to tell yourself why you can't do what God has told you to do. It will always sound logical. But logic and God are two totally different entities.

God's ways are higher and will always be higher than our ways.

Your natural man if you allow him to lead will cause you to do things that you never needed to do. You can worry and fret all you want and create gray hair, but you don't need to.

You may have only a portion of what you need for a situation, but God will take a little and make a lot of abundance out of it for you, and you will have some leftover.

We hinder God's ability to work miracles in our lives *when we only see and move in the natural realm*. God always wants to do *more* for us.

The multitude had been with Jesus all day getting healed of all kinds of maladies, diseases, and sicknesses. Although they were all healed now, they were not going to look forward to a day's journey back into the city (remember they came on foot out of the cities, and Jesus was in a deserted place).

Another reason the multitude would not have wanted to go back to the city was that it was a late hour, and it would have been dark by the time they got there. The stores would have been closed as well!

Doesn't Jesus think of everything?

Notice Jesus said, "You give them something." All God requires is that you give something, and he will multiply it enough so that it ministers.

All the disciples had were five loaves of bread and two fish, and they were looking at a crowd of five thousand plus women and children. In the natural, that is a lot of people to feed with only five loaves of bread and two fish.

Remember God's ways are higher than our ways, and his thoughts higher than ours. Jesus was thinking in the higher realm. That is where God wants us to live—in the higher realm. Thank God we can learn his ways and thoughts as we grow in the knowledge of him. We can go out into the world and be a blessing in the kingdom, benefiting its growth.

The first thing Jesus tells his disciples to do (he is thinking in the supernatural realm):

1) Bring them here to me... What do you have to bring to God?
2) Then Jesus commands order by taking authority over the situation. He tells them to sit down on the

grass…sit down and chill (he gets them comfortable). Psalm 23:1–3 says, "The Lord is my shepherd I shall not want. He makes me to lie down in green pastures, he restores my soul" (NKJV).

3) He took the five loaves and two fish.

4) He blessed and broke and gave the loaves to the disciples, and they gave to the multitudes.

You must first give what you have to God——your talent, your ability, your offering, your tithe. Then and only then will he take it. The only thing you have to offer God is yourself. He will then bless you and equip you.

Malachi 3:11 comforts by saying God will rebuke the devourer for your sake. God will take something from you, even when it belongs to him already, and then give more back to you, multiplied.

He will break you (this may take a while for some people).

And then he will give you back an anointing so that you can give to the multitudes; he will increase your wealth, your anointing, whatever you give him to use.

Only until God takes us and breaks us will we have anything to give to a hurting world and those in need.

Verse 20 says, "So they all ate and were filled" (NKJV).

You are going to experience a great deal of pressure at times; and unless God has blessed what you are doing, what you have, what you are, who you are, you are never going to be able to accomplish all that God has for you to do.

Notice in verse 19, Jesus gave the multiplying food to the disciples and the disciples gave to the crowd.

The crowd witnessed only one thing. Twelve men were handing out food, and there was no deli around, and they were getting fresh bread and fish from nowhere.

Now each of the twelve disciples had something to give, and when the crowd was full, each received a basket full of provision as well.

God will multiply what you give to him so that you in turn can give it away in order that (1) your work will remain and (2) you will always have more than enough to meet your own needs.

The disciples (twelve) each gave what they had and afterward each one had a basketful for themselves! God doesn't require that we have a lot to give him, but he does require that we give him what we do have.

God can turn a little into much. For he is able to give us exceedingly abundantly above what we can think or ask.

We must not be limited by what we think we have: "I will never be able to do anything for God. What do I have?"

It's not how much you have. It is not about you. It is all about God and what he has and what he wants to do.

Trust God with what you have. Let go of it… Trust him to do the miracles, signs, and wonders through what you give to him.

You will never see the miracles until you do.

4

Where Is the Love?

The apostle Paul beautifully describes God's character in 1 Corinthians 13. The first two words of insight are *patient* and *kind*. Let's stop here for a moment.

Walking with God leaves very little room for error because the path or road with God is narrow (Matt. 7:14).

If we would be truthful with ourselves, most of us would have to say that we sometimes miss the mark regarding patience and kindness.

But we can be encouraged in knowing that when Jesus is describing the road as being narrow, he is referring to it as a progressive walk. It is great to know that our God is so patient with us, and he doesn't expect us to get this overnight.

If we want to be like God, act like God, and please God, we will have to find out what God is like.

We know that God is love according to 1 John 4:16.

We can say, "I love you," or "I love them," or "I love God"; but sometimes, it is only vain talk spoken so carelessly since we really haven't mastered the interpretation to love someone the way God loves us.

I am talking about the God kind of love, the love that is unconditional, the kind of love that puts others' needs before your own needs and desires. When God offered Jesus as a sacrifice, it wasn't because he needed us, but rather we needed him and because he so loved the world. God reconciled the world to himself, and we are now ambassadors for him to spread this good news and bring heaven to earth (Matt. 6:10).

In order to be like God, we must actively have residing within us his love—a love that forgives every offense although our emotions are not necessarily wanting to. But we need to because God made us to fellowship with one another and not be independent from one another (Acts 2:42, NIV). They (the believers) devoted themselves to the apostles' teaching and to the fellowship. In the Greek, *fellowship* means "social intercourse, association, communion, contact, intimacy." They were joined together by love; they stayed in touch with each other, making sure needs were met. They encouraged each other by doing this. They felt love from one another.

Let me clarify something. If someone continually abuses you, misuses you, slanders you, etc., it is still required of God to forgive that person. But it doesn't mean that you have to reconcile the measure of intimacy you once shared. That is not wisdom. Forgive them, and don't allow them to remain in your inner circle of activities.

Don't confuse forgiveness with feelings. Forgiveness is not always a feeling. It is an act of faith.

Paul describes love as what it is and what it isn't, what it does, and what it does not do.

God's word in black and white gives guidelines for our lives. We have a choice to obey him and enter into the fullness of life; or we can do our own thing, disregard specific commandments or advice, and miss out on enjoying life to its fullest here on earth. God reminds us if we love him, we will keep his commandments.

Love is patient (enduring).

Enduring something or someone isn't always comfortable, especially if it's a someone who is rubbing you the wrong way! But by faith continue to endure and soak in God. Eventually, the wrong way will get all rubbed off, and it will eventually not have any effect on you. That is the idea—getting all the junk rubbed off us!

Love is also kind. In other words, it is benevolent, it is considerate and generous, it is loving and courteous. It means having or showing a tender and considerate and helpful nature, warm-hearted, characterized by mercy and compassion. If you are kind, then you have a desire to go about helping people. The "me, mine, and ours" syndrome is abolished.

Jesus was the perfect example of love. Didn't he go about doing good?

He healed people. Doing good will have a domino effect in your life.

So besides enduring people and situations (without complaining) and being a helpful person, we move on to the next requirement of love.

Maybe if we conquer patience and kindness, the other requirements will become easier to practice. We have to practice love. In Romans 5:5 (KJV), the love of God has been shed abroad in our hearts by the Holy Ghost, which is given to us. But through practice, we allow the love in us to flow out of us. Sometimes, we have to pump and pump the well of living water where that love dwells.

Paul said, "Love is not rude" (NIV).

I had the opportunity and temptation to be rude one day at the grocery checkout. The man in front of me had already checked out, and he was continuing a lengthy conversation with the girl at the register and the grocery sacker. I was becoming impatient and noticed the checkout to my left was becoming available in a couple of moments, so I anticipated moving my items. However, the Holy Spirit began to speak to me that it would be rude to do that. I then waited patiently until she decided to scan my items.

Love does not envy, does not boast, and is not proud.

When walking in love, you will not be discontented or resentful by another's possessions, qualities, or blessings.

Have you ever known someone who looked as though they "had it all"? Sometimes, we look at the outward appearances of people and think that they have everything. They have a mansion, expensive automobiles, maybe a live-in cook, gardeners, housekeepers, private airplanes, and the list goes on and on. But what about their happiness? Are they really fulfilled? Is God's fruit being produced in them?

True prosperity is not just having "things" and doing "things." A person can own the world but lose his soul. The person who appears to have it all could be the most miserable person on the planet. Maybe their mate is unfaithful. Maybe their child was born with defects. Maybe constant strife is involved in their relationship. Maybe the parents don't have unity and love with their children.

I have seen people who have everything as it were but are not serving God with all their heart, soul, strength, and mind. They are too busy with their "toys." They are into themselves rather than Jesus and his kingdom.

> For what benefit is it for a person to
> gain the whole world, yet forfeit his life?
> (Mark 8:36, NET)

There is such a thing as having true prosperity. It is having fulfillment in your mind, will, and emotions. It is walking in good health and enjoying material blessings as well. Most of all, it includes a healthy spirit, one which is in love with Jesus. It includes having unity with your family and spending quality time with your family. It is simply enjoying life to its fullest in every area. It is about quality relationships.

Which would you rather have, the things of the world or true prosperity? You can have both.

Matthew 6:33 promises if we seek first the kingdom of God and his righteousness, these "things" will be added to us.

In 3 John 2, we are told that God desires us to prosper in all things just as our soul prospers. We need to get a kingdom mind-set; then God will give us these temporal things. After all, "things" will one day pass away, but our souls are eternal.

Love does not show off; it does not blow itself up by bragging by patting itself on the back.

"Boy! I sure did preach a good message!"

> But the one who boasts must boast in the
> Lord. (2 Cor. 10:17, NET)

The Bible further reads in 2 Corinthians 10:18, "For it is not the man who praises and commends himself who is approved and accepted, but it is the person whom the Lord accredits and commends" (AMP).

God doesn't commend big heads.

It is up to God to do all the promoting.

Love is not self-seeking and is not easily angered (it is not irritated to the point that it becomes like a sore, red, and inflamed).

Did you realize that you can have a feeling of anger and show it by displacing an angry silence? There are some men that internalize, but I think a good number of women tend to internalize their feelings by entering a withdrawal mode. In many days past, I could stay silent for days if I wanted to. I have never been much of a talker anyway, so it didn't bother me in the least. But I have learned it is not about me.

I used to be famous for doing this to my husband, and my reason for this was to avoid conflict, but all it did was cause conflict. I have learned through practice to just let it go, and then I don't have to withdraw to avoid conflict. It took much practice!

Walking in love takes effort and practice. It is a journey, a road, but thank God the path of the righteous increasingly shines brighter and brighter. The way to keep from stumbling on that path of love is to walk in the light of God's word. When we speak God's word consistently to our situation, it lights up our pathway and works as a lamp to our feet (author's translation).

Love keeps no record of wrongs.

If every time you have an argument, let's call it a discussion, and you bring up things from thirty years ago, nothing has been accomplished. Your love walk has suffered a setback.

Everything that has ever happened to us whether good or bad is stored in our brain. Whether or not we want it, it's definitely in brain storage.

So when something unpleasant is constantly brought to our mind, the old brain activates the memory like it just happened. It becomes fresh in our mind and in return brings heartache. That enables strife. Where there is strife and confusion, there is every evil work. Don't give the devil place in your life. Strife, which is usually associated with unforgiveness is the number one area where our enemy gains an entrance of influence and deception.

Don't allow the devil to get his foot on you; your foot is supposed to be on him. Doesn't the Bible say that he is under our feet?

Ephesians 2:6 reveals God has raised us up together and made us sit together in heavenly places in Christ Jesus (KJV).

We have been placed in a position (heavenly places) in Christ Jesus *far* above *all* heavens (Eph. 4:10).

Ephesians 6:12 describes the evil ranks of authorities in the heavenly places, but bless God, we have been made to sit together with Christ Jesus in all his authority!

So we must allow the new man who is recreated in Christ Jesus to dominate our minds and our thinking because our actions follow. If something comes to your mind that has affected you, you bridle your tongue and don't speak it. You don't have to say everything that comes to your mind. I would like to sometimes, but I can't, and neither can you if you want to please God in your love walk.

Love is never glad with injustice but rejoices when truth wins out. Practice hating evil and loving righteousness.

If you love someone, you will be loyal to them no matter what the cost. You will always believe in them, always expect the best in them, and always stand your ground in defending them. Love always protects and trusts and hopes.

The word *loyal* means showing firm and constant support or allegiance to a person or institution. We need more loyal members in the body of Christ in order to affect a hurting world.

Leaking Vessels

The water Jesus spoke of in John 4:14 is the Spirit of God that springs forth, but remember it is also possible to spring a leak. You can accidentally or purposely allow the fountain of life—the well of living water to leak and escape through a crack. A crack is something that gives way under pressure or strain or to escape through a hole: a small, awkward, or unpleasant place or situation (Oxford University Press).

So we keep coming to Jesus; he said if anyone thirsts, "let him come to Me and drink" (John 7:37, NKJV). I don't know about you, but I get thirsty every day. Don't you?

Just as we often have to fill our tank with fuel which empowers our car, in the same way, we have to keep coming back to the "filling station of God" to get refueled. On a regular basis, we require more because we give it away ministering or maybe we leak joy under pressure of strain or through an unpleasant situation or place.

Our workplace can be an unpleasant place.

Our relationship with our boss can be an unpleasant situation.

Our family relationships can be unpleasant.

We can have pressures from our jobs, our children, our mates; there can be financial pressures that wear on us.

We can feel strained, mentally tired, and stressed out.

There are any number of reasons to spring a leak.

Because of this, we are inadequate to minister to the hurting, the depressed, the oppressed, and the sick. Why? It is out of the overflow or abundance of the Spirit of God that we are able to minister to those who are in need.

You can't give out what you don't have. You can give out, but it is not going to be life-giving. It is not going to have any power in it.

We must be filled up and spilling over to have enough for ourselves and enough to give away.

God knows exactly what we need because he sees our inward man. Does our attitude need an adjustment? Are we loving others as God loves us? We may suppose we are, but when we surrender ourselves and get alone with God, he will reveal to us how we really are. We may not always like what he shows us. But the good thing about it is he won't leave us there. He will come in and pour in and love on us and fill us up with his presence! When we come out of his manifested presence, we will be feeling totally different than the way we felt upon entering.

God never sends anyone away empty. Without fail, he gives more than enough in order for us to give some of it away. Sometimes, you will have the opportunity to give his presence away almost as soon as you get it. Let me explain how this can happen.

We are in a safe environment when we enter the presence of the Lord. I call it a safety zone. No one can hurt us, no one can abuse us, no one can pull on us, no one can tug on our patience, no one can call us for advice about their lives. We are in a safe place with God, and we are having a glorious time.

We are becoming filled with his glorious presence, his anointing, his power, his ability, his joy, his peace; it is *wonderful!*

Then we float out to our cars (if we are soaking at church), or we float out of wherever we have been soaking in his presence, but then the phone rings. Someone is at the hospital getting stitches. Maybe our job is experiencing a problem… What do we need to do about a certain situation?

Immediately upon leaving a peaceful atmosphere, we begin giving away some of God's grace, some of God's peace, some of God's healing power.

Already we are leaking, and suddenly, we are not floating anymore. Remember we are not of this world (Phil. 3:20), but we are sure in it, and everywhere we go, people are hurting and are in need. That is why we need the overflow or spilling. The overflow's purpose is to reach out to those who haven't been in the presence of God.

We have to drink for other people. *Glory!* It's fun to drink of the living water of God.

I heard a woman tell a story one time about marinating or soaking cucumbers in vinegar solution. She gave such a beautiful analogy of a cucumber soaking and how we can do the same thing to become something totally changed.

If you place a cucumber in a vinegar solution and leave it there long enough, it will become something different. It will become a pickle. It will not become a pickle overnight or even after a few days. But if it is left in the solution long enough, it will become pickled and taste like a pickle and look like a pickle.

It is the same way with people. God is the solution, and if you place yourself in him and remain in him and soak long enough, you will become what he desires you to become in him. You will be like him. Your mind will begin to think differently. Your attitude will begin to change. You notice more love in your heart toward someone that you once had a difficult time loving. You gradually become like the pickle in the vinegar, the result of a changing process. You are no longer a cucumber but a pickle!

> But fill the followers of God with joy. (Ps. 70:4, TLB)

Revived!

I have seen people come to River Soaking walking in with such tired faces, so stressed from the day. I've been the same way.

I've seen people walk in looking like they could beat up their mate. I've felt the same way.

I've seen people who were so thirsty that if they didn't drink some water soon, they would not make it. I've been the same way.

We all have felt like that at one time or another.

They always leave though full of God with such peaceful looks on their faces.

I have seen them crawl out of the sanctuary so drunk on the new wine they can't even walk. They drag themselves or crawl out. Suddenly, they have forgotten their problems. The stress has lifted because they surrendered their minds to the Holy Spirit. In return, he took their stress and cares and gave them what he has-*peace*.

I am not saying that the problems went away. When they went back to work the next morning, though, they had a different attitude about the situation. They have confidence in their God now that they didn't have or in some cases had lost sight of. Instead of frustration on the job, they now have a renewed hope. The peace that the Holy Spirit gave them the night before is going to secure joy for their day. It is going to give them the patience they need, the strength they need, the wisdom they need.

God knows exactly what you need before the need arises.

Isn't that what happens when you drink alcohol or wine? If you drink too much, you become drunk. You can't talk and make sense. You can't walk, and if you can walk, you can't walk straight! When you drink in the natural, you get silly and usually obnoxious. Who wants to be like that? That kind of drunkenness destroys lives.

When you drink in the natural, you forget your troubles.

When you drink in the natural, you begin to laugh at the silliest things because you lose all of your inhibitions. You feel free…but because people have done this, many have lost their family or employment security. It has brought them to ruin.

Another thing with drinking in the natural is that you wake up with a hangover, and it hasn't benefited you in the least. Maybe it helped you to relax so that you could forget your pain and not have to deal with anything for a while. But the pain always comes back. The hurt always comes back. Then you feel you need another drink, and it becomes a cycle.

But when we drink of the Spirit, we are, by faith, drinking in God's presence. We are taking a humorous drink. When God's presence touches something, it changes! Even though we might not "*feel*" anything happening at the time or moment we begin drinking, please know that *something is happening in your spirit.* Sooner or later, you will begin to experience a change in your emotions. What once often upset you will not upset you anymore. Why?

Because something has happened inside you.

When you surrender your time to God, drink of his Spirit, and meditate on his Word something happens. Without realizing it, more of God's ways and thoughts are taking over your life, and less of your ways and thoughts are there to mess it up.

> The person who has my commandments and keeps them is the one who really loves me; And whoever really loves me will be loved by My Father, and I too will love him and will show (Reveal, manifest) Myself to him and make Myself Real to him. (John 14:21, AMP)

7

❧

Soaking and Crying

God began this "drinking" renewal in Toronto, Canada, in January 1994. Oddly enough, that was the same month and year that I was diagnosed with breast cancer. I have to admit that I didn't take it very well. The cancer, that is.

It was through God's wonderful grace and his mercy that he began drawing me to himself. I listened to worship music and began soaking by myself (at this time, I didn't know it was termed "soaking in God's presence"). I was just spending time alone with God in my bedroom. I would wake up every morning and spend hours with him in prayer, reflecting and reading the Bible. I worshiped him like I had never worshiped him before, and he suddenly began pouring out of me through poems and songs. A year and seven months later, I began to teach the songs leading children in worship at my church.

Already, the Lord was causing something good to come out of my soaking time.

I would read the poems that God gave me, and they would give me such comfort. They gave me enough comfort and strength that by his grace, I was able to recover from a mastectomy and three months later undergo reconstructive surgery. I didn't need radiation or chemotherapy. For that, I am so thankful.

In January of 1994, I found a lump in my breast and had a sonogram. I was diagnosed with breast cancer. At this time, I couldn't say that I "knew God" like I know him now. In fact, I can tell you I didn't *know* God at all! By that, I mean I did not have an *intimate*, closely acquainted, familiar, private, and *personal* relationship with him. I prayed of course, but there was no *intimacy*. When you have intimacy with someone, you really know the person. You know what they will do and what they wouldn't do. You know what they like and what they don't like. No one would be able to convince you otherwise, because you *know* them. You've had a positive and personal experience with them. You have faith and confidence in their words.

In order to be intimate with someone and know and experience them, you have to spend time with them. That is how I know my husband. I have spent time with him, and I know him. I know his character. I know what he likes. I know what he expects from me. I have spent one on one quality time with my husband. I have a personal experience of him. If he told me he would do something, I would believe him and expect the results of what he had promised. It is the same way with God. That is what I meant when I said I didn't know him. To know him is to love him. To love him is to keep his commandments, and to love him is to love others as God has loved us. When you love someone, all you want to do is spend time with them and be alone with them. You want to share your feelings, talk, and communicate with them. I didn't know God at all! I believe that I wanted to, and I thought I loved him. But I soon recognized I was consumed with the cares of this life—not with him and his desires—at least not enough to forsake all others and other things that would draw me away from him.

The night before the day of my surgery, I attended a service at my church. Our guest speaker gave a prophecy to me, and I will never forget it. He told me God had healed every cell in my body and not to be afraid. I must believe God and not believe the report of man.

What was I to do? Surgery was already scheduled, and the sonogram couldn't lie! I had seen the X-ray! All I knew was that I didn't want to have cancer and lose my hair. I didn't want to die. I didn't know the Word (I hadn't experienced it). I didn't have the faith to believe 1 Peter 2:24. I didn't know God well enough to believe him that I would live and not die. That is the honest truth.

I went to Toronto in 1995 with a group of women from my church. It was a wonderful time and experience in God. I would get prayed for in the prayer line, I would fall under the power of God, I would feel like I was glued to the floor and wouldn't be able to get up, but all I did was cry.

I would cry because of what I had been through with the breast cancer. In fact, the day before my scheduled surgery, the Lord gave me these words:

> I've got a long day ahead of me tomorrow
> I'll be glad when it's over and I'm through
> Jim said he'd be glad to take my place
> But it's something that I have to do
> For me it's not a pleasurable thing
> But I've made the final decision
> I have to follow through with this

I couldn't believe it was in remission.

Oh, how many times have I considered those words? How many times have I wished I could go back and do it all over again.

I would do it differently; I would not have had my breast removed. I would not have had to go through reconstruction. I would have been able to avoid all of the pity parties that I gave myself.

I think I wore my husband out with my crying, but through it all, he was right there beside me all of the way, listening to me cry, listening to me complain and murmur about how I looked. He would then tell me how beautiful I was and listen to me ask what seemed to be a thousand times, "Why did I do this?" He comforted me every time and just loved on me, assuring me that it didn't matter to him. He loved *me*, and he was so thankful I was alive and still with him and our two children.

No one really knew what to say to me, and I didn't feel that anyone understood what I was going through. I felt so alone. My husband and children (they were grown and away from home), and pastors showed their support in all the ways they knew.

I began reaching out to God for his help. I began to tell him how much I loved him and that I was thankful to him for sparing my life. I asked him to forgive me for having the surgery. (God was meeting my need according to the position of my faith.)

If you are not sure how to draw near to God and develop an intimate relationship, I suggest that you first begin by thanking him for loving you so much. Begin counting all your blessings and thanking him for them and his awesome goodness toward you. That is called worship.

How many times did I ask God to forgive me for not believing for a miracle, for not trusting the words of the prophet! Believe in the prophet, and you will prosper! (Of course, the prophet should have a history of accuracy, and he did.) Do you realize that it only took one time, and God heard me and forgave me? I had so much hurt and pain and anger on the inside of me. A part of my body was now missing that didn't have to be missing. I was angry with myself, and all I could do was cry. I cried for about a year.

So naturally when our group of ladies from church decided to go to Toronto, I was the first to sign up. I was so excited! I was tired of crying! I wanted this "laughter" that I kept hearing about. I had never experienced laughter like that. I had never known the joy that was noised from people who invested their time in what was known as the Toronto Blessing. I wanted it for sure. I *needed* it! I *wanted* it!

And while in Canada where all the laughter and joy abounded, instead

I would cry wondering what I did to bring this awful thing upon me (cancer);

I would cry because God had been so good to me and spared my life;

I would cry because I loved God;

I would cry just because;

I would cry because I couldn't "feel" anything spectacular;

I would always cry. I wanted to laugh;

I would cry because I couldn't laugh.

People all around me were laughing and seemingly experiencing God and his joy.

I wanted that more than anything. I wanted to experience laughter because that is what everybody seemed to be doing in God's presence. Besides, I love to laugh! A cheerful heart is a good medicine (Prov. 17:22, ASV), and I wanted to take a big dose of it!

What I wasn't realizing though was the fact that I *was* receiving. God simply had a lot of work that he had to do in me, and the crying was part of the process—sometimes a process, depending upon its nature will take quite a bit of time to complete. God had to reach deep within me and get all the junk out of me. Tears were the only thing that came out, but it was through those tears that the healing came.

Ten years later, I was still soaking and still crying. I wanted to experience God's joy. After all, isn't there a feeling of great pleasure and happiness in God's presence?

Surely by now, I would be able to laugh. God gives us the desires of our heart when we delight ourselves in him (Ps. 37:4). I was feeling great pleasure, but I still wasn't *laughing*. Now ten years later (at the time of this writing), I still cry but not because I can't laugh. It's because of how much I love and adore God! I cry and don't always know why.

Let me encourage you for a moment.

On the day of Pentecost when the 120 were gathered in the upper room, they were all *filled with the Holy Spirit*. People began accusing them of being drunk because of the way they were talking and stumbling around. But they weren't drunk on wine, they said. They were drunk on the Holy Spirit! It was a prophecy spoken by Joel that in the last days God would pour out his Spirit on all flesh (Joel 2:28, NKJV).

This outpouring of God gave Peter such boldness (you are really bold when you get drunk, right?) that Peter preached about Jesus, and about three thousand souls were saved just from that blast of the Holy Ghost (Acts 2:41). Peter was saying what Joel prophesied about the outpouring of the Holy Spirit was promised to them and their children and to *all who are afar off* as many as the Lord will call (Acts 2:39, NIV). God has kept his promise, and we were now again experiencing his Holy Spirit outpouring.

When God's presence comes upon you, there's a possibility you may want to resist him. Personally, *I like it because I have put forth a great effort* in learning to receive. I have reached out to him and asked so many times for his presence. I now am able to immediately recognize his companionship.

As I explained in an earlier chapter, the extent of time shared with someone is the determining factor in recognizing their voice. It is easier to hear God's voice (which is the Holy Spirit inside you) when you sit alone, just waiting for him to speak to you, waiting for him to give you an answer or idea about something you're desiring. You may get ideas coming to your mind during that time. You may experience a vision. It's possible to hear something you've never heard before. God communicates with us through our physical senses.

In the realm of dreams, God often speaks as well. It may require time and patience, but you will learn a unique language in which God communicates.

When we're asleep, our minds turn off, and that is the secret to understanding and receiving God.

Our minds work all day with life's tasks. It's no wonder we have so many dreams.

It's possible to have a sweet taste in your mouth or smell a certain odor. A smell of frankincense and myrrh has been a normal for me, sometimes popcorn. (I find feathers in my home in random places. God is showing me that I have angelic protection.)

Maybe you will think about someone you haven't thought of for a long time. That's usually the Holy Spirit urging you to call or check on them. It's imperative to trust God with what you are experiencing during your private times with him. It might seem silly to you, but as you grow in intimacy with God, it will make absolute supernatural sense. It's how he communicates.

> Glory in his name; let the hearts of those rejoice who seek the Lord! (1 Chron. 16:10, AMP)

It's Time to Get Serious

God spoke to my heart to hold a service each week for the purpose of soaking and seeking God's presence. For whatever reason, not too many people seemed to be interested in it. But there were four of us including my faithful husband and another couple. Soon afterward, another couple began coming and continued to be faithful. For about six months, we met upstairs in the Prayer Center playing soft worship music, loving on God, and allowing him to love on us while asking for his sweet presence. Guess what happened during the first six months? After ten years of somewhat intermittent soaking and seeking God's presence at home, I began to laugh! If I didn't know better, I would say I couldn't believe it. But I could. It was definitely worth the wait! It was an inexpressible joy.

If you are seriously desiring God's presence, you must seriously seek him. I was not thirsty enough to seek God's presence on a continuous basis. I had been seeking him part time, and all I received from God was a part-time relationship. Seek him full-time and receive full-time benefits!

I have seen times when I and others were unable to get off the floor. It felt like we were glued to the floor. We were so saturated in God that his presence was heavy on us, and we were almost helpless until the anointing lifted. One night before River Soaking was to begin, I was praying in the sanctuary and seeking God about the Soaking Service and what he wanted to do. I felt impressed he wanted intimacy with us and to dance with some, to take others away to his secret chamber and speak songs of love to them (Song of Sol.). He desired to overshadow us as with Mary in the New Testament. The Holy Spirit desired to impregnate us with a holy desire for travailing prayer (groaning) and birthing.

We want what God wants, the main agenda having souls saved and living the abundant life. Travailing prayer is the way the apostle Paul accomplished it. An example of travail is in Galatians 4:19. Paul was speaking to born again Christians whom he had travailed through prayer into the kingdom, yet they were acting immature in Christ. Paul wrote to the churches in Galatia, "My dear children, for whom I am again in the pains of childbirth, until Christ is formed in you" (NIV).

What Paul was saying was he had a burden upon him that needed to be released through prayer. Birthing things into the spirit realm is much like birthing babies in the natural realm. There is a feeling of heaviness, a burden that will only leave through deep, inarticulate sounds of pain or despair. I have seen people, including myself, in a natural birthing position, sometimes bent over or lying on my side curled up. It is a laborious effort. But after the delivery, I was tired yet in a state of calmness and ecstasy, as a woman experiencing her newly born infant; she has brought forth something new.

That night, God showed me what to share with the group. The Holy Spirit wanted us to begin to allow the Holy Spirit to move upon us through groaning and to respond to him through travail. When he comes upon you in this way, it's all you can do.

By the end of the service, some ladies were groaning and having fun doing it! After I dismissed everyone, I went into the restroom, and about four or five ladies were in a bent-over position, travailing and trying to walk out of there. It's not something you do just because you want to. The Holy Spirit must fall upon you through travail. It's usually always after you have been with the Lord and/or have been in intercession that this will come about. It is now a frequent occurrence in intercessory prayer for some of the women to travail during our prayer times at church. It is always as the Spirit gives unction.

I had so much hurt, pain, stubbornness, and sin in my life. It took ten years for me to allow God to operate, removing all of the things that were holding me back from totally surrendering my life to God and his will for my life. Now I understand to seek God about decisions and proceed, and if it's not for my good, he will provide another direction.

> the hand of our God is upon all them for good who seek him but his power and wrath are against all those who forsake him. (Ezra 8:22, AMP)

9

Helping Others

In order to do the works of Christ, we must be filled with the Holy Spirit.

Ephesians 5:15–18 says we are to walk or live uprightly or diligently, redeeming the time, because the days are evil. Don't be unwise, but understand what the will of the Lord is. Be not drunk with wine...but be filled with the Spirit (author's translation).

The Holy Spirit is the power within us that causes us to triumph in Christ Jesus.

It is not that we can be filled one time, and that's it. We can spring a leak.

We need to be replete—well supplied and fully supplied with the Holy Spirit.

If we are not satisfied fully in God, what makes us think we can go out and effectively help others?

How can we be a witness of God's love and power if we don't *really* know him?

Your outflow of love to others is limited to your revelation of God's love for you.

Jesus asked his disciples, "But who do you say that I am" (Matt. 16:15, NET)?

Do you know who Jesus really is?

Who do you say that he is?

Do you know without a doubt that he loves you and you are special in his sight?

Do you know him well enough and are you confident enough to speak for him? Are you able to share with others about who he is and what he will do for them? Are you confident to share what Jesus has already done for them?

Do you say that he is *the healer, the strong tower, your shield and buckler, the "need supplier," the all-sufficient one, the one who gives peace that passes all understanding, the one who cares about your every concern and knows about every detail of your life?*

It is so easy to get out of sync with your intimacy with the Lord. How easy it is to gradually decrease or decline in the amount of time we spend with Jesus. All it takes is a couple of days, and we are out of our routine. The early morning rising to pray and soak is now used for getting to the job because we have a deadline to reach. Because we have a deadline to reach and have to get to the job earlier than usual, we become tired. Now we can't even spend some time at night with him because we have to get up early to go to work!

Maybe you are used to getting up early and spending quality time with Jesus, but perhaps something or someone is now requiring your attention. You have to miss that morning of intimacy. The day prolongs, and for some reason, you don't have the patience that you need. You don't have the flow of encouragement that is needed for someone. Slowly and gradually, your amount of intensity in your relationship with Jesus is declining. You don't want it to. Real situations have come up, and you are required to handle them. What do you do? You are tired, and now you don't even feel like going to River Soaking once a week.

I realize it is hard to find time to spend quality time with the Lord when you have small children who demand your undivided attention.

What you can do, though, is train your thought life. Train your thoughts to stay on Jesus as much as possible. Think on things that are pure, things that are pleasant and beautiful and of a good report (Phil. 4:8). During the day as you prepare your child's meal, think on those things. Think about how much God loves you even if you don't "feel" it at the time. God loves us whether we "feel it" or not. God doesn't change. He loves us at all times. Our feelings have nothing to do with our relationship with God or his word.

I have not always "felt" saved, but the Word says I am because I have accepted Christ as my Savior, and that is good enough for me. If I don't believe that with my heart (not my feelings), I won't be saved. It is a faith thing, and faith is the thing that pleases God.

Think about the beautiful sunshine that warms you on a spring day. Begin naming and counting all the blessings that you have. You will discover you have more than you realize. Ask God to give some "special time" openings in your schedule to be devoted to him. I wish I had known to do that when my children were small. The only time I thought about God was when we went to church on Sundays and Wednesday nights. I would pray before I ate my meals, and I would pray to God before I went to sleep. I would pray with my children before they went to sleep and on the way to school every morning. That was the extent of my relationship with the Lord.

That is the advantage of having grandchildren! What you didn't do with your own children you have a second chance to do with your children's children!

I have tried to teach my grandchildren all of the things that I didn't teach my own children. Oh, I taught them about God, and I thank God that I was sure to have them in church regularly.

But with my grandchildren, I have had more to give and invest into their lives. I have had the wonderful opportunity with the two younger grandchildren to teach them about soaking and desiring the presence of God. The only reason I wasn't able to be that example to my older two is that I didn't know enough about soaking in the presence of God when they were young.

You have to reach the children when they are young and impressionable in order to leave a Godly impression with them. My two older grandchildren love the Lord, but I didn't have the pleasure to teach them about the presence of God.

When I would talk to my youngest grandchildren (at the ages of five and three), I would try to make it fun for them. With the boy, I would gather all of his little bears that he keeps at our house, and we would place them on the bed in a circle, facedown. I would tell him to help me explain to them that this is the way to worship God. We would take turns bowing before the Lord and telling God that he is holy and we love him. We would then take the bears and help them to "bow down" to God.

On another occasion when our youngest granddaughter had spent the night, the next morning, I put a soaking CD on and didn't think anything about it. After feeding her breakfast, we were walking toward the bedroom, and I said, "Katie, the Jesus music is on. Let's soak."

We lay on the bed cuddling together, both of us with our eyes closed. After a few minutes, I began to worship the Lord and ask the Holy Spirit for more of God's presence. I asked the Holy Spirit to "keep coming." I looked at her, and with her eyes still closed, she raised her hands and held them as if she was holding them out to contain something. She then began to slowly wave her hands back and forth as if to give the Lord a wave offering.

I was so blessed, to say the least.

> I love those who love me, and those who seek me early and diligently shall find me. (Prov. 8:17, AMP)

10

Investing

In a previous chapter, I mentioned the Holy Spirit began flowing through me in poems and prophetic songs.

About a year and seven months after having cancer, I began playing the keyboard and leading in the singing for the small children at my church. It is amusing to me as I think back and realize how God called me to work in the children's ministry at my church.

I happened to be walking by the room where the children met on Sundays. It was in the Fellowship Hall, so I didn't have many reasons to be walking by that room on Sunday mornings.

The children were already in the class and were singing, but they had no music to accompany them. The teacher was trying her best, but as I walked by, my heart went out to them. I felt so bad that they didn't have any music. Of course, the Holy Spirit spoke to me and reminded me that although I was no master in playing (to say the least!), I could play for the children. I could at least play enough to help them have some fun and help them minister to the Lord and he to them.

I spoke with my husband about it and asked if he minded me being absent from the service to play for the children. Next, I asked the children's teacher if it would be all right *and if* they wanted me to help. The answer was overwhelmingly, "Yes!"

I began the following Sunday morning. That was August 1995, and I continued for over ten years working with the children, playing the keyboard and leading them into worship. I would tell them God is with us and to focus on him.

God rewards faithfulness and will add and bring increase to what you do. Later on, God unveiled his desire to minister his presence, on occasion through short prayers and the laying on of hands.

They are thirsty even at such a young age.

When asked, "Who wants to feel God's presence and his power?" they all raised their hands, and they all received God's touch. I explained to them how they could receive him at home as well. All they had to do is just ask the Holy Spirit to give them "more."

What a tremendous blessing to be used by God and to be able to invest in and have something to give to others. God has so wonderfully blessed me with the opportunity to be able to teach all four of my grandchildren praise and worship. For they all have graduated Children's Church where I led praise and worship.

What the enemy meant for harm, God turned around and caused good to come from it. The enemy stole from me and tried to kill me, but God spared me. From out of my despair, God drew me to himself. For that one thing alone, I would change nothing.

No, it was not God's will that I have cancer, because he had already healed me through the stripes on Jesus's back (1 Pet. 2:24). It was up to me to believe it and to receive it, but my faith level wasn't there yet. I wasn't at a place in God where my faith level would preserve me from surgery. God is loving and merciful. He met me at the level of my faith and honored that. God uses doctors, and I believe that he guided the surgeon's hands and the anesthesiologist to bring me back from under the influence of prolonged anesthesia.

God was with me again when the plastic surgeon removed a muscle from my back to benefit reconstruction of a new breast. Although God gave me a very speedy and beautiful physical recovery, it was my *mental* recovery that took so long. It was obtaining the special possessions of God and the renewal of God that I struggled with for so long.

How patient is our heavenly Father! He loves for us to humble ourselves in approach to him demonstrating total dependency upon his grace and mercy. It is the same way with our children, isn't it? Even though they may have made an inferior decision or rebelled a judgment call, we still love them. But a possibility remains *they* may feel distant until finally coming to receive restoration and a parental blessing.

How much more has our heavenly Father (who loves us more than we could ever love our own children) bestowed upon us all things that (are requisite and suited) to life and godliness, through the (full, personal) knowledge of him (2 Pet. 1:3, AMP).

After all, isn't that what we are after?

> And you will seek me and find me when
> you search for me with all your heart.
> And I will be found by you, declares the
> LORD, and I will restore your fortunes and

will gather you from all the nations and
from all the places where I have driven
you, declares the LORD, and I will bring
you back to the place from where I sent
you into exile. (Jer. 29:13–14, NAS)

11

Let the Holy Spirit Do His Job

> However, I am telling you nothing but the truth when I say it is profitable (*good, expedient, advantageous*) for you that I go away. Because if I do not go away, the Comforter (*Counselor, Helper, Advocate, Intercessor, Strengthener, Standby*) will not come to you [*into close fellowship with you*]; but if I go away, I will send him to you [*to be in close fellowship with you*]. (John 16:7, AMP)

Isn't it good to know that we can rest our faith in the fact that Jesus *did* go away and that he is still connected with us through the Holy Spirit?

Jesus told his disciples that he had accomplished his goal and his purpose in the earth. He had come that we might have life and have it more abundantly (John 10:10). He overcame all of the temptations of Satan so that we could overcome when we are tested—so that we can live an over-coming lifestyle.

There is no reason for any born-again believer to live in anything less than a comfortable lifestyle. Jesus came that we might have plenty of anything we need.

Paul said it like this, according to the *Living Bible Translation* in Philippians 4:19: "And it is he who will supply all your needs from his riches in glory because of what Christ Jesus has done for us."

Because of Jesus and what Jesus has done, Paul said if we require something because it is essential or very important, God will supply or make it available for us. Notice he would make it available for us, but something else is important. We must have faith in who God is. We must have faith in his reward to receive anything (Heb. 11:6).

God will supply our need according to his abundance, his wealth, his fullness.

Jesus told his disciples that his job was over and about to end. Although Jesus would not be with them in the flesh anymore, someone else would come to take his place. (That person being the Holy Spirit.) Jesus stayed connected with them through the person of the Holy Spirit.

The word *connected* means to be related in some respect. Not only is Jesus now our elder brother and our intercessor; he has also "connected" us to the heavenly Father through the Holy Spirit. He has joined us together so as to provide access and communication with our Father God. Jesus is the intercessor between God and man. He has reconciled God and man.

What Jesus accomplished through eleven men (Judas betrayed him) he can now accomplish through any and all who believe on him and receive the Holy Spirit to dwell within.

Don't be a Judas and sell out to God. Don't give up your inheritance in God for the world's riches. It will cost you your life. It will ruin you. You will not be a witness; rather you will be a failure in this life.

I pray that you will receive the revelation truth that Jesus, the one who lived on this earth and performed miracles and died on a cross and was resurrected in three days, is now living inside of your body through the person of the Holy Spirit.

He wants to complete a work in you. According to Philippians 1:6, the Holy Spirit will continue developing that good work and perfecting and bringing it to full completion in you (AMP).

The Holy Spirit will lead us into all truth, and since he is the Spirit of truth, we must depend on him to lead us in God's word for the renewing of our minds. The word of God will bring us into perfection (maturity in Christ).

We are also instructed in 2 Timothy 2:21 (AMP) to purge (cleanse, separate) ourselves from sins, carnality, and fleshly desires that will separate us from God. We are to be vessels of honor, having steadfast faith and purified hearts. Then we will be useful for the Master's use and made ready to enter into the work that God would have us to do.

We are able to do this only through the working of the Holy Spirit.

Some people will try to change themselves (either their character or their habits) but only become frustrated because they are not experiencing any change in their lives. Why is this? *They* are trying to do it by themselves. Life is hard without the Holy Spirit's help. That is why he is referred to as our helper. *He* helps *us*. Actually, he does all the work. *We* are not supposed to please God *by* our works. That doesn't impress God. What impresses God?

God is so pleased when we ask him, "Make me pleasing to you. Place me into the center of your will."

The Holy Spirit gets excited when he hears those words!

He is well qualified to bring you to the place of change. If he can't, then we are in big trouble! But bless his holy name he is more than able.

He is the potter, and we are the clay (Isa. 64:8). The clay is supposed to be pliable for the potter, and when it is, the potter is able to create any kind of vessel he chooses—as long as the clay remains pliable.

The clay will remain compliant as long as it remains in the potter's hand. If it is left alone, it will become hardened, and the potter will not be able to use the clay.

I mentioned earlier that people sometimes become frustrated when they don't readily see a change in their character or habits. They want to be changed without bearing effort, but it is a process! After the potter has fashioned us and places us in the fire, we jump out because we can't stand the heat—finding we must return to the spinning wheel once again to begin the molding process. That is why we become frustrated. We suppose we are a finished product, but we are only half done! It actually becomes a cycle.

It is a cycle until we come to the place of complete desperation and full-time surrender to the Holy Spirit.

Godly character is perfected in pressures and trials of this life.

We could save ourselves a lot of hardships if we would simply concede to the Holy Spirit's continuous leadership and direction. God wants us to be mature (perfect) people in this world who know how to bring heaven's fullness to earth.

The Holy Spirit accomplishes this kingdom work through every *willing* person.

Because the Holy Spirit dwells in every born-again believer, we can, as believers, do greater works or greater quantities of works than Jesus did. Jesus was only one person, but now his person resides in many.

Each and every born-again person has been given a call (some are called to ministry) of reconciliation. Along with the call, God provides a gift or gifts according to the particular call. We all have been called to testify of God's goodness and love toward us. But some have been called to a particular area of ministry, and God's gift or spiritual endowment will make room for that call. In other words, through the individual, God will flow in a divinely given gift and produce the necessary results. Galatians 3:8 reads that God spoke to Abraham the gospel saying in his seed all nations would be blessed. The seed is Christ Jesus, and we are in Christ Jesus. Therefore, we are blessed and responsible to spread this wonderful news to the world, thus making this world a better place.

Praying for the Sick

> How God anointed and consecrated Jesus Christ of Nazareth with the Holy Spirit and with strength and ability and power, how he went about doing good, and in particular, curing all who were harassed and oppressed by the power of the devil, for God was with him. (Acts 10:38, AMP)

> And these attesting signs will accompany those who believe in my name...they will lay their hands on the sick, and they will get well. (Mark 16:17–18, AMP)

Attesting signs means that it provides clear evidence that those who believe in Jesus's name will lay their hands on the sick, and they will get well.

First of all, we know that it is always God's will for us to be healed. That has to be settled in your heart and mind (3 John 2).

Jesus is our example, and the Holy Spirit dwells in us to carry out the examples of Jesus.

God anoints us to heal.

In Matthew 10:8, Jesus gave the apostles orders to heal the sick or bring a cure, and in Matthew 28:19–20, Jesus told them, "Make disciples teaching them to observe everything I have commanded you and I am with you all the days perpetually, uniformly and on every occasion" (AMP).

Notice that God not only anointed Jesus with the Holy Spirit but also with strength, ability, and power.

Jesus walked in love 24-7 with the fruit of the Spirit hanging all over him at all times. He was perfect and complete in God.

If you want to see people healed, the love walk is a requirement, for without faith, it is impossible to please God, and faith *works* by love.

God calls some in the church to be used in the *gifts of healing*, which is a special calling along with the working of signs, wonders, and miracles. That is when the Holy Spirit heals instantly or performs a sign or wonder or miracle… something you can't explain how it happened. It is a wonder. (I wonder how that happened!)

The gift of faith will also be in operation along with these gifts.

But every believer *has* scripture to back them up. Lay hands on the sick, and they *will* (future tense) recover or get well. That is a promise from God. They will; healing is a process, and it begins the moment your hands touch someone in faith. It can come in an hour or a week later, but it will come. Go to the doctor, and get some antibiotics. Take one four times daily, and probably you will get well (I would rather believe God. It saves money!).

After I was baptized with the Holy Spirit with the evidence of speaking in tongues, I was so on fire. I wanted to heal people. Nobody told me to. No one told me that God was going to use me in the gifts of healing. It just came natural to me. I thought everybody did it.

A good place to start praying for people is with your family. That is what I did.

One of the first people I prayed for was my son. He was two years old at the time and had ear infections quite frequently. The doctor told me that he had another infection, and he would have to place some tubes in his ears in order to protect his eardrums.

That night when my son was asleep, I went into his room with my opened Bible and laid it on his chest. At that time, I didn't know any healing scriptures, only that I needed a miracle from God and believed that he could give me one. As a simple act of faith, I opened the Bible and placed the scriptures on top of my son. It's amazing how God will accommodate a believer's faith!

So I simply placed the opened Bible on his chest and began to pray to God. I said, "God, you know that we don't have the money to pay for this operation if he needs it, and besides that, I don't want to have to go through the ordeal of doing it. I ask you to give Addam a miracle."

Immediately (Addam was asleep), he began to clear his throat from all the drainage that was being released from his ears! From that time on, he never had another ear infection.

Another member of my family was my sister-in-law, Dawn. She was only a young girl at the time. She was in bed with tonsillitis and fever. I happened to come to their house, and when I saw her, I asked her if I could pray for her that

Jesus would heal her. She said, "Okay," and I laid my hands on her and prayed. She immediately began to feel better and told her sister and mother who were in the room with us.

I then left.

Later on, I found out as soon as I left, my mother-in-law and my other sister-in-law began to convince Dawn that she really wasn't feeling better, that it was just in her mind. Dawn told me when she heard those words, she began to feel bad again. She was young and didn't know any better. But since that time, Dawn and all her family have come to believe in the healing power of Jesus.

Just tell them that God loves them and wants them well and ask (be sure to ask) if you can pray for them. You can say something like, "I'm not sure why, but God wants me to pray for you. Is it okay?"

I wanted to lay hands on any sick thing that moved. I thought I was supposed to heal everybody. But not everyone wants to be healed, and you are not called to heal everybody.

God wants you to be sensitive to the Holy Spirit's leading.

There are certain people with certain gifts flowing through them that can reach certain people.

The more often you pray for people, you will find areas of the body that you have more success with healing. Also the more often you pray, the stronger the anointing becomes and the bolder *you* become. The boldness is a confidence in God that is referred to as the gift of faith in operation.

God has called me to heal in the areas of the sinus, brain tumors, knees, stomach disorders, breast cancer tumors, and bone calcium and growth disorders.

He also has anointed my hands to bring healing by rubbing or massaging the muscles of the back and shoulders.

I have prayed for several women with breast cancer, and tumors were dissolved. Shirley, my pastor Shirlene's mother, had a severe stomach disorder which I believe was the result of ulcers. I laid my hands on her stomach. My pastors were there, and my husband, Jim, was there praying. I asked the Holy Spirit to hover over her stomach and create a new lining in her stomach. She had an endoscopy the next day, and the doctor said that she had the stomach lining of a fifteen-year-old. Let me tell you for sure that it definitely was not me but the Holy Spirit *working with me.*

My pastor once called me to the altar to minister to a man having one leg quite a bit shorter. I thought, *Why me?*

But he told me to lay my hands on the man's foot and command the leg to grow out in Jesus's name. I did, and the leg grew out. I was just as surprised as the man was.

I had no knowledge of healing back then. I believed that God would heal, but I had not been brought up in a church that believed in healing miracles.

It is imperative that you get to the place that you hate evil and love righteousness. You must hate sickness and recognize its origin. Ask God to give you a burning desire to see people loosed from their bondage. You must hate sickness and disease because Satan is the author of it, and it cost Jesus his life.

Hebrews 1:9 (speaking of Jesus) says, "[You] love right and hate wrong, so God, even your God has poured out more gladness upon you than anyone else" (TLB).

Besides the Holy Spirit, Jesus's strength came from his joy (which is in the Holy Ghost). The joy of the Lord is our strength. If we are downcast, heavy burdened, sad, mad, discouraged, etc., we won't have much of a drive to go about doing good and healing anyone, will we? Who in the world is going to believe us?

Again, be sensitive to how God might be wanting to use you. Maybe he wants you to speak some scriptures over the person. Maybe he wants you to simply touch them softly while releasing his anointing. You can pray over the phone by sending the word of healing.

Psalm 107:20 says God sent his word and healed them. God sent Jesus, the living word. God's word is still alive and powerful and active, so we can send the word through the phone.

Maybe God will tell you, "Do not touch them at all but only say to them, 'Be healed,' in the name of Jesus!"

Peter and John, in Acts 3, were going to the temple at the hour of prayer. It is a good thing to stay in a prayerful frame of mind. Stay prayed up. Pray in the Holy Ghost, building yourself up on your most holy faith (Jude 20). If you don't have faith in Jesus for someone to be healed, then it is possible the healing won't take place.

Peter and John weren't the only people going to the temple to pray that day. If you make yourself available, God will divinely set up circumstances in your life to help someone.

The lame man wanted some money from Peter and John, but Peter told him to get up and walk, and Peter lifted him up, and he did walk. What a testimony! Because of this, about five thousand believed on the Lord.

You never know what God has in store if you will simply make yourself available.

You have to hate sickness.

The stronger you hate it, the stronger you are going to be expecting people to be healed when you pray for them. If you pray for someone and are expecting to see a miracle or some kind of result and you don't see one, tell the person with boldness that they *will* be getting better soon.

You have to believe it yourself in order for someone else to believe it especially people that are in the world.

If you are ministering to someone, tell them that the word of God is alive and powerful and sharper than a two-edged sword (Heb. 4:12) and that it was released or imparted into them when you laid your hand on them. Anything that is alive is continuing in existence or use. It is alert and active.

Therefore, the word of God is continuing to perform in them until it brings a cure. It is continuing to be alert and active. Be sure to know the word so that you can use it if that is the way the Holy Spirit is moving.

Jesus was anointed of God, who went about doing good…

Get out into the marketplace or wherever your world is and speak kind words. Do good deeds. Speak blessings over people the babysitter, grocery clerk, your doctor, the dry cleaner, etc. (I have prayed for my doctor before, as well as his nurse concerning healing for her mother and for help from God for a business matter.) Everyone usually accepts prayer.

You can begin a conversation over the weather and end up healing someone or praying for their needs and become a blessing to the kingdom. It is all about the kingdom. Be kingdom minded… Hate sickness. Always be available and full of the Holy Spirit and faith.

Example:

> Now there was a certain disciple at Damascus named Ananias; and to him the Lord said in a vision, "Ananias." And he said, "Here I am, Lord." (Acts 9:10, NKJV)

A. Be available.

1. A certain disciple named Ananias…you could be a certain disciple.

2 He answered *correctly*, "Here I am, Lord. I'm available."

3 Verse 13 says Ananias shared his heart with the Lord…that he was afraid of Saul… Evidently, he had an open and ongoing relationship with the Lord. He didn't go ask anyone if they thought it was God's will… He knew God's voice.

4 God will not condemn you for sharing your fears with him. He will comfort you and give you the boldness you need.

5 Ananias was obedient to lay his hands on Saul and spoke short and sweetly, "I have been sent by Jesus so that you can receive your sight and be filled with the Holy Ghost."

B. Keep it simple.

1. Saul was already learned in the scriptures and the law, but because he was deceived, he didn't know the simplicity of the Gospel. When the scales fell from his eyes, he could see the light… Jesus *is* the Son of God! He knew the law but didn't know Jesus. *There is a difference, and it will show.*

2 Increase success by increasing in strength. Paul had success after staying several days with the disciples of Damascus. He immediately began proclaiming Jesus was the Son of God and increased in strength by the attesting signs. He convinced people that Jesus was the

Son of God through the signs, wonders, and miracles that were performed in his name. The more you speak of Jesus, the more you hear, and faith comes by hearing.

C.   Be sensitive.
    1.   Acts 9:33 says Peter found a certain man paralyzed.
    2   Peter simply told Ananias the truth of God's word...that Jesus Christ has healed you (1 Pet. 2:24). Get up and make your bed! After eight years in bed, he was healed instantly. It doesn't say that he laid hands on him, only spoke the Word.

The centurion told Jesus to simply speak the Word and his servant would be healed... There was no need for Jesus to come to his house. Jesus was amazed at his faith. When was the last time Jesus was amazed at your faith?

D.   Be sensitive... Ananias's healing led to Tabitha's believing friends to call for Peter in hope for a miracle.
    1.   Acts 9:36–40
    2   Get rid of doubt, doom, and gloom; and stay focused on Jesus, the truth, the answer.
    3   The room was filled with widows who were focused on the things, the garments that Dorcas made. Had they been focused on Jesus, they might not have had to send for Peter. Is it possible they were focused on the fact that she wasn't going to make any more coats? The believing friends were sending for

the answer. Doubt will *focus* on the fact, and faith will *focus* on the truth.

4   Peter knelt. When was the last time you knelt before the Lord? Knees denote strength, so to kneel would symbolize giving up your strength and calling on a greater power to enable you to perform, in this case a miracle.

5   Peter focused on life and not death... The Bible doesn't read that he looked at her a while and then prayed... He might have gotten over into unbelief as well.

6   As he turned toward her, he spoke to her. He first sought truth and then dealt with fact.

7   Truth: Jesus came that we might have life (John 10:10).

Jesus said to heal the sick and raise the dead (Matt. 10:8).

Fact: Tabitha was dead.

Truth is greater than fact.

Peter only said, "Tabitha, arise" (KJV). "And turning to the body he said, "Tabitha, arise." And she opened her eyes, and when she saw Peter, she sat up (NKJV).

I believe she saw Jesus in him. People will see Jesus in you too. It is called the grace of God. Only then did Peter touch her; he took her by her hand and helped her to her feet. Then he allowed her believing friends and the widows to come into the room. Perhaps the believing friends were praying for Peter at the same time he was praying. Prayer is always involved in the work of the Lord.

So in prayer, Peter not only was empowered to raise her from the dead; but God showed him how to do it.

I believe it was Smith Wigglesworth who would take a dead body and stand it up against the wall and command it to walk in Jesus's name. On occasion, it took him several times, but the dead assuredly began walking!

It is time to see faith in action and see some action from our faith!

13

⤛⤜⬥⤛⤜

Are You Serving God's Purpose for Your Life?

Have you ever wondered why you were created or what you were supposed to do? God spoke to Jeremiah and profoundly informed him (Jer. 1:5): "Before I formed you in the womb I knew you, before you were born I set you apart, I appointed you as a prophet to the nations" (NIV).

Jeremiah was called to be a prophet to the nations.

Not everyone has been set apart by God to be a prophet. But everyone who has been born has been appointed or assigned to be a special someone—to carry out a special mission in this world.

God told Jeremiah that he knew him, which is to say that he recognized him. God recognized ahead of time, before he formed Jeremiah in the belly of his mother, that he would use him for a specific purpose and in a specific period in time. God has recognized you as well but perhaps hasn't revealed to you a specific task to accomplish.

I will clarify: not everyone has a specific calling, as did Jeremiah.

An individual should follow their heart in the way they are gifted.

Maybe you were born to be a prophet, maybe a school teacher, a janitor, maybe a doctor, maybe a mom, maybe an evangelist, or maybe a grocery checker. Some are recognized and appointed to the five-fold ministry of the Lord Jesus Christ; some are not.

We all are called to a ministry...the ministry of 2 Corinthians 5:20. We are Christ's ambassadors, representatives, promoters of the fact that God so loved us that he poured our sins into a sinless Christ and in exchange poured his goodness into us. Everyone can minister that in any domain in life

What is the reason for which you were born? Why are you here in this period of history? Has God ever let you in on his plans for your future?

Jeremiah had a *specific* mandate or an *official* order for the use of his life. But we know that God does have plans for all to prosper, plans to give hope, and plans to give all a future...something yet to happen.

You are significant. God chose you in Christ before the foundation of the world (Eph. 1:4). According to our God-given gifting and talents, we have a predetermined plan for a successful life. Quoting Francis Frangipane, "At the proper time the miracle of God's activity will emerge in your life like precision clockwork."

> Even as [*in his love*] he chose us [*actually picked us out for himself as his own*], in Christ before the foundation of the world, that we should be holy (*conse-*

crated and set apart blameless in his sight
even above reproach, before him in love.
(Eph. 1:4, AMP)

Since God did all of this for us, he is not going to leave
us to just float around in this world so that one day we can
die and go to heaven!

God has a future for each of us, but we need an expec-
tancy in our heart that the future is going to be good—
because God said it would. Remain optimistic.

We belong to God, anyway; why can't we trust him and
put our faith in his sovereign ability to do us good? We have
his word that he will not only give us hope but will give us a
future that is good, one that will not harm us. Why can't we
just trust that? A suitable future.

Since God is not a respecter of persons, each one of us
has the promise of a successful future, a flourishing future, a
prosperous future. But how do you recognize your purpose
and reach your destiny?

1) The first thing you must do is humble yourself.
   Determine in your heart that no matter what God
   tells you to do, you will do it. Surrender your will
   to his *known* will for your life, his written word.

If you are not walking in what you already know to do,
God will not trust you with something else.

Delight yourself also in the Lord (the
previous verse already instructs to trust
in the Lord and do good) and he will give
you the desires (requests or petitions) of
your heart. (Ps. 37:4, AMP)

So do what you know to do. Make yourself pliable and soft toward God.

2) Resist the temptation to doubt God's word. The devil will do everything in his power to direct you into unbelief of what God says about you or what God says to do.

What did he do with Eve? He convinced her to doubt God... The word of God has to be absolute in your heart and mind and never be compromised. It must be independent of all doubt. You must have a resolve in your heart and mind to obey and follow after God, never speaking words of doubt or unbelief. It is your enemy. If you falter and speak doubt, quickly call those words back and repent to God.

Hebrews 6:12 (KJV) says, "Be not slothful, but followers of them who through faith and patience inherit the promises." You can't be slothful or lazy in the kingdom of God and expect to inherit the promises of God. You must keep faith working for you, believing God. God doesn't approve of laziness or slothfulness... A lazy person will not run the race, and therefore, he can't expect to win the prize. He is disinclined to work or put forth the effort that is required to obtain.

Hey, operating in faith and patience takes effort. Anyone can doubt. Anyone can be impatient. But patience is a fruit of the Spirit. It is to be something that you bear. Not everyone can be long-suffering (which means to be patient). Not everyone can be slow in avenging wrongs. Not everyone endures; not everyone can be consistent or persevere— steadfast—only those who make the decision in their heart and mind: "God, not my will but yours." And every time an occasion arises for you to become upset because your feelings were hurt, don't allow that opportunity to pet your flesh and make it feel good. You will know when your flesh is upset; it will hurt! Do not be lazy. Exercise your faith. Keep your mouth shut, and go off in another room if you have to so that you won't respond wrongly. How do I know this?

Second Thessalonians 3:10 says, "He who does not work shall not eat" (TLB).

Titus 1 warns those who are unemployed because of laziness or idleness, "you are able to work but are useless."

Have you ever seen a lazy ant?

Proverbs 6:6 instructs us to "Take a lesson from the ants, you lazy fellow. Learn from their ways and be wise. For they have no king to make them work yet they labor hard all summer gathering food for the winter. But you, all you do is sleep. When will you wake up?" Let me sleep a little longer. Sure, just a little more. [That means in Hebrew to be drowsy] (TLB).

One translation says "a folding of the hands," which means to be idle. Isn't that true? If your hands are folded, are you using them? And as you sleep, poverty creeps upon you like a robber and destroys you. (*Poverty* is from a root word in the *Hebrew* meaning "destitute," which means to be extremely poor and lacking the means to provide for oneself).

Have you ever seen a street person and wondered how they got there?

Perhaps there are all kinds of reasons for that, but if that person simply tried to avoid activity or exertion, he is just plain lazy and wrong. It is unscriptural.

It is one thing to be handicapped and unable to work, but to be able to work and not do it isn't right. When God drove Adam and Eve out of the garden of Eden, he placed a mandate upon their lives. Adam was to till the ground or work by the sweat of his brow.

He was to be diligent and productive. Eve was to bear children, which is a job in itself! I believe it was always God's will for a woman to nurture the children and make a home a pleasant place and be a helper to the husband. But in our society now, so many times, it's necessary for the wife to work outside of the home and help in that way as well.

If you are a single parent in need, you might have to go to work to feed yourself and your children.

3) Pray to God about your future. He is the one who has it all planned out. You are the one who has to walk it out. Ask God to reveal a plan and purpose for your life, and then begin thanking. He will speak to you in a number of ways. He is not limited in ways to reach you. *You* pray. Don't depend on somebody else to always pray for you. Grow in personal intimacy with the Holy Spirit; that's *his desire for you.*

First John 5:14 says we can have confidence that God hears us when we pray and will answer when we pray according to his will.

In Jeremiah 33:3, God instructs to call him...cry for help, and he will answer you and show you great and mighty things, fenced in and hidden which you do not know (do not distinguish and recognize, have knowledge of and understand) (AMP).

Is there anything you are wanting knowledge of, wanting to understand? *You call to God, and he will answer you.*

He will speak to you through a prophet. First Corinthians 13:9 says, "For we know in part and we prophesy in part" (NKJV).

A true prophet will prophesy only what he hears from God. God doesn't tell a prophet everything about your life in one sitting. If you were to learn everything about your life at one time, you wouldn't trust God anymore. You would go after it and pursue your destiny instead of God. You would be pursuing your future with a passion instead of pursuing God with a passion. Anytime I have ever been promoted in the spiritual realm, I was pursuing God, just doing what I knew to do.

God imparts to us what we can believe as we are able to believe yet stretches our faith at times.

Matthew 8 shares the story about the centurion, a man of authority, a man of humility and compassion. He understood Jesus could speak the Word only, and his paralytic servant would be healed. The centurion could have sent any of a hundred people to Jesus for help, but he came himself on behalf of a servant. He was a kind man, a compassionate man. He could have sent away his servant because of his handicap and replaced him with another servant. He didn't have to waste his time and energy on a servant. We must never get too busy in our pursuit to have time for someone else. Because that is what the kingdom is about—people. That is the reason Jesus died—for people.

Notice that Jesus rewards the centurion's faith with a "Go! It will be done as you believed it would" prophecy. If Jesus said those words to you, what would you receive? "It will be done just as you believed it would." What are you believing? *Are* you believing? Without faith, it is *impossible* to please God. In other words, your faith would be impotent... It would not be producing results. Your faith would be sick... It would be shooting blanks.

The centurion believed in the omnipotent deity of Jesus; he understood what authority meant, not only in the natural but in the supernatural realm.

1) Check your love walk.

Faith only works by love. If you are not walking in love, your faith is hindered from working. Your faith won't do anything, because it can't. Your faith couldn't remove a mountain if it wanted to if you're not living a lifestyle of love toward God and people. God tells us to love him, keep his commandments, and we are to love others as he has loved us.

So in order to please God, we must have faith, and in order for our faith to be producing and pleasing to God, we must be operating in love. So you can't be pleasing to God unless you are walking in love. One is dependent upon the other, because sometimes you can't walk in love without faith!

Sometimes, God will let us practice on our relatives. The people who should love us the most and the people we should love the most sometimes become a battleground of mastering the love walk.

What is love? God informs us in 1 Corinthians 13:4 (NIV) that love is *patient*... There's that word *patient* again. Notice that the word *patient* is the firstfruit listed?

I believe when the fruit of patience or long-suffering remains effective in our life, the rest of the love walk won't be as challenging. Love doesn't run its course simply by being patient; the next fruit in line is *kind*. It is one thing to be patient, but you have to be kind. Who wants to be around a mean, patient person? No, you want to be around a patient *and kind* person. Love is kind, it does not envy, it does not boast, it is not proud, it is not rude, it is not self-seeking, it is not easily angered, and it keeps no record of wrongs.

Love does not delight in evil but rejoices with the truth. It always protects, it always trusts, always hopes, always perseveres. Love never fails (1 Cor. 13:4–8, NKJV). It never ends, because God is love (1 John 4:16), and we know that God will never end or fail.

14

If You Can Begin in Faith, You Can Finish in Faith!

> God so loved the world that he gave his
> only begotten son that whoever believes
> in him shall not perish but have eternal
> life. (John 3:16, NIV)

What love the Father has for us that no matter *who* believes in him shall be saved. No matter how far away from God you might be, there is always hope that your relationship with God can be reconciled. Now we tend to think that some sins are worse than others. Some might be inclined to think that the person who kills a baby *deserves* everlasting punishment more than the person who lives an adulterous lifestyle, but blasphemy against the Holy Spirit is the *only* sin that will not be forgiven by God.

The truth is, we all need to receive God's forgiveness.

That is the beauty of God. Jesus's blood has covered every sin imaginable. What matters to God is that we repent of our sins and receive forgiveness. God's gift to the world through his Son, Jesus Christ. That is what our loving Father is all about. He is after the person's heart who is truly penitent and fully in love with his Son, Jesus. God "thought the *world* of Jesus" and expects us to as well. He *gave* Jesus *to* the *world,* and he wants us to *give up the world* or the affection of its system for Jesus. I don't think that is too bad of a trade, do you?

If God can have your heart, he can work in and through you. It is your heart's condition or motives that are of importance to God. "And I am convinced and sure of this very thing, that he who began a good work in you will continue until the day of Jesus Christ right up to the time of his return, developing that good work and perfecting it and bringing it to full completion in you" (Phil. 1:6, AMP).

God loves enough to pursue us through the tender wooing of the Holy Spirit. He wants us to be the best we can be while we are on this earth.

Right now would be a good time to stop and thank God for your salvation, forgiveness of sins, and the grace he so generously supplies to you every day. It is just for the taking. Take what belongs to you. Everything Jesus suffered was for your benefit.

Did you notice that it is God who began and is going to finish the work in us? We can't do it ourselves, so relax.

Learn to rely on the Holy Spirit. He is the one who is responsible for us. All we have to do is respond to him in obedience.

Proverbs 4:23 (KJV) reads, "Keep thy *heart* with all diligence for out of *it* are the issues of life."

Jesus called the Pharisees the offspring of vipers, and he asked them how they could speak good things when they were evil (wicked). They were full of labors, annoyances, and hardships. He continued to warn them, "For out of the *fullness* (the overflow, superabundance) of the heart the mouth speaks" (Matt. 12:3, AMP). In other words, out of your mouth will flow whatever is in your most inner being or the center of your being, the person you really are.

I was meditating about the tremendous love that God has for me, and it almost blew me away! His love suggested to me that God cared about my eternal soul—more than he cared about Jesus and what he would suffer in order for me to be able to spend eternity with him! Let that soak in for a moment.

That might raise some religious eyebrows, but think about it. God was so absolutely in love with the world and human race that he refused to leave mankind in the condition he was in after Satan's subjugation. Whomever you submit yourself to obey becomes your master. That is why Satan took over the earth. Adam submitted to Satan's deception by eating of the tree of the knowledge of good and evil. God said not to; Satan said it was okay to. What would you have done in that situation?

In effect, Adam handed over his dominion and authority and gave it to Satan because he now changed his obedience from God to Satan. Now Satan could rule the earth *and* man. But God, as usual, was prepared. He continued with his love of creation, and his will would continue as planned.

Adam deliberately disobeyed God, but Eve was deceived into believing something false. It's not recorded that God told Eve not to eat of the tree of the knowledge of good and evil. Adam must have told her himself, and his words didn't carry much weight. He was not functioning as the head of the woman or even being a spiritual influence to her.

Eve proceeded to eat of the forbidden fruit. She then gave it to Adam, who was with her, and he ate without hesitation. At least Eve was bold enough to confront the snake!

At this point, Adam should have taken his authority to dominate the situation on her behalf; Adam was not watching out for his wife.

Ultimately, God drove them out of the garden paradise because of their disobedience. Disobeying God will always cost you something. I don't think the fruit was worth it. I don't think the fruit would have appeared good enough for them to be willing to exchange their living standards for the rest of their lives—let alone throughout eternity.

I once saw a church sign which read, "Forbidden fruit creates a lot of jams."

Can't you imagine the conversation between Adam and Eve as they were packing up to leave paradise? I feel sorry for Adam.

I absolutely love Hawaii. My husband and I would rather be there than anywhere else in the world. There are plenty of gorgeous places on this earth, and we have been to a lot of them, but to us, Hawaii is just a special place. We call it paradise. We have never wanted to leave there to come back home. We just love it. If our kids and grandkids could come see us once a month and stay for a month at a time, we would probably move over there. But we love our family too much. I would have to challenge the thought of never returning to Hawaii, "the paradise place."

But can't you picture Eve staring at Adam as they left the beautiful garden of Eden? They couldn't even return once a year for a vacation. God placed an angel to guard the entrance (Gen. 3:24).

Now they had to go to work. Adam had to feed the family, and Eve had to start having babies and sewing clothes. She was now not only a mother, but had a profession—she was a seamstress. She held down two jobs. Following population, she began to show others how to make their own clothes. Now she was a teacher. Now she had three jobs—all because Adam conceded his authority to the enemy. If men would exercise spiritual authority over attacks of the enemy upon their families, I believe there would be fewer divorces today. There would be fewer heartaches, fewer regrets, fewer families without moms or dads.

Jesus was doing just fine in heaven. Talk about "living the life of Riley." Jesus was literally living "the life of Jesus." There were no cares up there. No one having to be healed all the time. No demons crying out to him to leave them alone. No Pharisees or Sadducees to deal with. No "experts" in the law to have to correct and teach all of the time because of their cunning, trapping questions. There were no fishermen to have to train to become fishers of men. There were no storms to awakened Jesus from sleep. Jesus didn't have to learn a trade and do physical construction labor in heaven. He didn't have to spend forty days and forty nights in a wilderness with the beasts, fasting so that he could come forth with power to overcome the temptations of the devil.

The list goes on and on about the life Jesus had in heaven. Jesus *was* the abundant life in heaven. He had unlimited, uninterrupted communion with his Father. Can you imagine the joy he experienced?

Then God and Jesus planned earth's creation—further preparing a garden paradise, "and there he put the man whom he had formed" (Gen. 2:8, KJV).

The man was placed in the garden and was given the responsibility to care for it and maintain it. It has always been

God's will for man to work. Men, if you have a family to support and are physically able to work and are not doing it, then you are out of God's will.

God then told Adam that he could eat of every tree of the garden, except of the tree of the knowledge of good and evil, because "in the day that you eat of it, you shall surely die" (Gen. 2:17, NKJV). Now to me that doesn't seem like a lot of rules or laws to follow. All Adam had to do was (1) tend the garden and (2) don't eat of the tree of the knowledge of good and evil or he would die.

Sounds good to me. Two things to remember: Take care of the garden, and don't eat of the tree of the knowledge of good and evil, or I'll die. Okay, I can do that.

Don't you know God was pleased with the creation? The first chapter of Genesis tells us that God thought everything he made was good.

So we know that man was a good thing. I know some women think, "What happened to them?"

I can imagine some men responding with a reply, "Women happened to them!"

While God was showing Adam the garden in all of its splendor, he emphatically warned Adam not to eat of a specific tree. There were so many more from which he had to choose, just not *that* one. Since Adam was alone and God thought that it was not good for man to be alone, God would make him a helper suitable for him (Gen. 2:18, NIV). So God brought to Adam every beast of the field and every bird of the air and all of the cattle for Adam to name. Whatever Adam called the animal or bird, etc. would be its name. (Wow! I believe Adam exercised every brain cell in his head. I'm wondering what would happen if we would do the same). But Adam had still not found a helper comparable to him.

It doesn't matter what the circumstances appear to be. Remember that if God has spoken something over your life, don't give up thinking you have run out of options. God is not limited in his ability to create. Adam had thought he had seen it all. Everything God created had been displayed for Adam's opinion—almost everything!

God will do the same for you. If he has to create something, he can and will *if* you will only believe. Adam was believing God because he didn't know not to! He didn't know how to be in disbelief. All he had ever known was God. He had no reason to doubt God. He didn't even know what doubt was yet.

God put Adam to sleep, and while he was sleeping (don't you know that was wonderful sleeping?), God took one of Adam's ribs and made a woman (to build, obtain children). But God "formed" (through the "squeezing into shape") man (Strong's Greek/Hebrew Definitions).

Husbands, your wife was designed to be "built" up. She needs it every day. Build her up, and make her feel important and loved.

Stress sometimes takes effect upon the husband who has responsibility to support a family. He is doing all he knows to do, but sometimes, it seems it is never enough. Wives, there are situations occurring during your husband's workday that you don't know about or *need* to know about.

Although your husband is designed to manage a certain amount of pressure, don't add to the stress. They sometimes get enough of it from their employment. God knows I have added to my husband's stress at times, even when I didn't know I was doing it.

Wives sometimes think their husbands need to be corrected or "squeezed into shape." Wives, God is already forming your husband. Remember that God has a future for him.

Therefore, remain in faith and in prayer, and you will benefit from his good future. If you think he needs reshaping, have patience and let the Holy Spirit do the job. He can do it a lot faster than you can.

The Holy Spirit is reminding me of a movie I once saw about a man's hands that looked like large hedge clippers, and out of a hedge or even hair, he could form the most beautiful and perfect-looking object in only seconds. Think of what the Holy Spirit could do with your husband. Maybe your husband needs to change his ways; maybe you *just think he does*. Ask God about it. It could be that it's not your husband with the problem. Could it be you?

> When God created the garden of Eden
> He knew in advance
> What we would be needing.
> But he felt so inclined
> To make Man a place
> A place so beautiful
> To begin the human race.
> Now the man, Mr. Adam
> And his lovely wife, Eve
> Did enjoy the paradise
> Until the day Eve was deceived.
> Once that happened
> Their whole life changed.
> God removed them from the garden
> Into dominion where the devil reigned.
> But God in his love
> Set a course in which Man could rely.
> A plan of salvation
> Where the soul never dies.
> When God made Adam

To leave the garden
Provision was already made
To supply him a pardon.
Although Adam sinned
God's love never stopped.
He would crush Satan's head
And after Man's repentance
His sins would be dropped.

What a loving God we serve. I fall more in love with him every day because of what he has sacrificed for me and my family. I have peace and joy knowing that I will be able to spend all of eternity with my husband, children, grandchildren, great-grandchildren, my parents and grandparents, and the list goes on and on. How wonderful and comforting to know that I will never be separated from God or my family throughout eternity—all because of what God sacrificed for the world (John3:16).

God so loved us he was willing to send his only begotten Son, Jesus, into this world.

Jesus so loved God he was willing and obedient to leave heaven and become implanted by the Holy Spirit into the womb of a young virgin. God's prophecy to "crush Satan's head" came to pass through Jesus's death, burial. and resurrection (Gen. 3:15).

Through the devil came every temptation known to man, but Jesus overcame them all so that *we* can overcome every temptation that comes to *us*. This produces a victorious lifestyle.

Jesus was scourged and beaten resulting in thirty-nine stripes. I read a doctor's account of Crucifixion and its effect on the body. The flesh on Jesus's back would have looked like stripes of ground meat.

During our tour in Israel, my husband and I noticed in a church a picture of Jesus made of stained glass. What managed to capture our memory of it all these years later was the awful sight of his missing teeth. He was beaten and bruised beyond the look of a human being. Isaiah 53:5 says, "But he was wounded for our transgressions. He was bruised for our iniquities: the chastisement for our peace was upon him; and by his stripes we are healed" (NKJV).

The blood he shed on the cross was for the remission of our sins.

God had told Adam not to eat of the tree of the knowledge of good and evil, for in *the day* that *he ate it,* he would surely die. God *knew* that Adam would disobey him.

Adam did eat of the fruit of that tree, but he didn't *physically* die that day. He lived about another eight hundred years or so. However, Adam died *spiritually.* God meant that he would be spiritually dead on the inside and would be eternally separated from God. You are a spirit, and you live in a body. Your body might die, but your spirit (and soul) will live forever because it was made after God, who is a Spirit. Your spirit is going to live forever. Choose for yourself who you will serve.

It is the *sin nature* that has to be dealt with. Everyone that has been born from the time of Adam and Eve has been born with Adam's sin nature. That's why we must be born *again* (John 3:3).

That is why the new birth, called being born again, is so important. Accepting (believing) in your heart Jesus's death, burial, and resurrection, and confessing him as your Lord and Savior will literally bring transformation to your spirit man. You will then become a new creation and equal the *nature of God.*

Second Corinthians 5:17 states, "If anyone is in Christ, he is a new creation: the old is gone, the new has come" (NKJV).

Once you accept and trust Jesus as your Lord, you become born again. It is like you never have sinned! You become like Adam and Eve were in the garden of Eden *before* they sinned. Once you receive Jesus as your Lord, you are brought back into fellowship with God, and you are no longer separated eternally from him. God *gives* you a gift, and his name is Jesus.

There is the probability that you will still sin again. God already thought of that too and made provision for us through his Word. First John 1:9 says that if we confess our sins to him (it sounds like we will probably sin more than one time), he is faithful and just to forgive us our sins and to *cleanse* us from all unrighteousness (KJV).

Take advantage of it! When you sin, don't run away *from* God but run *to* him. He knows about it, anyway. All you are accomplishing by running away from God is having a guilty conscience and broken fellowship with the one who loves you. When you sin or do something that you know is displeasing to God (the Holy Spirit will let you know), simply ask God to forgive you of it in Jesus's name.

There is nothing hard about serving God. God has thought of everything for us, and his divine power has given to us all things that pertain to life and godliness through the knowledge of him (2 Pet. 1:3, NKJV). Get to *know* and experience God. Become acquainted with God and his ways. He is good, holy, kind, merciful, and full of compassion and forgiveness.

Trust me, he is so willing for you to know (experience) him as Abba Father. He is longing and waiting to become your daddy God.

Perhaps you're not sure that God loves you, or maybe you once felt his love, but because of the cares in life, you have grown away from him. It is very easy to come back and be reconciled to him. He is patiently waiting to restore friendly relations! Jesus has reconciled us to God through his death on the cross. Do you think God takes that lightly? God loves you at *all* times. He loves you when you think you are being good, and he loves you just as much when you think or know that you have blown it.

If you sincerely ask God to forgive you of a sin, he will forgive you because he said he would. He never says something he doesn't mean. Your salvation is of ultimate importance to God, and he went to great lengths to redeem you from Satan's dominion. If God had failed to pay the price of sin, man would spend eternity separated from our Lord. But if you are in Christ, eternal salvation belongs to you.

Second Corinthians 5:8 says that Paul encouraged the church at Corinth, "We are confident, yes well pleased rather to be absent from the body and to be present with the Lord" (NKJV).

What tremendous peace we have knowing that we will someday be with the Lord rather than eternal damnation. The spirit never dies. I don't like to think about people who have died without wanting Jesus as Lord and Savior. God offers a choice of life or death and exhorts you choose life. There are two choices, heaven or hell.

> Blood drops of the covenant
> Cascading down on us
> Sealing all the promises
> Jesus gave to the just.
> Sealed by his blood
> The robes are pure and white

Without spot and blemish
We stand with nothing to hide.
Blood drops of the covenant
They still continue to flow
We're covered by this blood
With an inward witness, we know.
With confessions of our wrongs
The blood continues to drop
Because of God's faithfulness
The flow will never stop.
Drops of blood
The sins they do hide
When to the Father
You confide.
Drops of blood
Covering the sins
And feelings of hurt
From deep within.
Drops of blood
Ring out the sound
Redemption's here
In the blood to be found!
Drops of blood
Continue to fall
So stay in its bounds
It covers all.

Please pray this prayer with me:

Heavenly Father, I come asking you to
forgive me of my sins.
I believe that Jesus is your Son, and he
died for my sins.

I believe that he rose from the grave and ascended to heaven.

I accept Jesus Christ, and I confess with my mouth that Jesus is my personal Lord and Savior.

Jesus, come and live inside me.

Thank you. Amen.

In Matthew 14:15–34, the disciples declare to Jesus that it is late, and the five thousand -plus women and children are hungry, and he should send them away to the village to buy food.

They are thinking in the natural, five thousand-plus women and children are here, it's late, the local Albertsons is about to close, and they have no food to eat.

Jesus disapproving of their lack of faith declares they do not need to go away to the village. Jesus thinks bigger than we do and always sees the larger picture. He told the disciples, "You give five thousand-plus something to eat." Jesus was teaching them to operate in faith, but they missed the hint, the *first* hint being "they do not need to go."

Jesus's desire is always for us to operate in faith. If we miss it, he still loves us and will provide more opportunities.

Faith is a way of life that pleases God. It's a daily learning and growing experience.

If the disciples would have just *tried* to do what Jesus asked, a simple command, "Give them something," they would have seen a miracle through their own faith. They would have been able to "go to the other side" during the next set of trying circumstances. Don't try to reason how God is going to meet a need; only believe.

Remember the disciples had just witnessed a miracle. Little did they know that Jesus was presenting to them another opportunity to use faith. All they were required to do was get into a boat and sail to the other side of the lake. This seems like a simple task: "Get into the boat and go to the other side." They were fishermen; they knew how to handle a boat, right?

Don't ever boast about anything you can do. No matter how trivial it may seem, without Jesus's involvement, you won't make it to the other side. Boast in the Lord instead.

Jesus told them to go, get into the boat, and go to the other side—three things to do.

He told them he would finish taking care of the crowd. Do you realize how potentially chaotic the scene could be with that many people? Ponder this: The crowd was full; it was now even *later*, and they realized the miracle that had just taken place. I'm sure they began to discuss it amongst themselves and began racing toward Jesus for a personal prophecy. Jesus saw in advance what was going to take place. Maybe that was the reason for sending his disciples away.

The disciples managed by now to all be inside the boat. Everything seemed to be going their way on the sea, especially since they had just partaken of a huge miracle. I imagine the twelve were tired by now yet pridefully unstoppable. Jesus was on a mountain alone, praying. But now the boat is in the middle of the sea with wind tossing it back and forth.

Here is another situation arising after Jesus told the disciples to do something.

About 3:00 to 6:00 a.m., Jesus went to them in the fourth watch of the night. Jesus was smart. I believe he knew that a storm was brewing and the wind was contrary. He knows when things are contrary to the way they should be going. He is always on top of things. God will let you sweat a little sometimes to allow you to see where you and your faith are. When it seems it is the fourth watch of the night and you can't handle it anymore, God says, "Good, I'll take over now."

Jesus is always aware of your situation, and Jesus is always on time, and Jesus will always demand you to use your faith... All he asks is for you to try.

Jesus came walking on the water, and they thought he was a ghost probably because they were so tired from fighting the wind all night. Have you ever been so tired from battling a situation that you thought you were feeling delusional? Although they knew Jesus was going to meet them, they never dreamed he would come to them walking on the water. In fact, they didn't think he would come at all. They assumed they would have to ride the storm by themselves and tell Jesus all about it the next day, or maybe they thought Jesus would show up in another boat. The disciples never considered another miracle was on the way because they were too focused on their problem—the storm at hand. Had they already forgotten about the food miracle and that Jesus would have told *them to do something*? They failed to recognize Jesus because he was operating in a different means of provision. Don't try to figure out God, just expect him to come.

Remember the five loaves and two fish? I don't think the disciples remembered. When you are facing a possible crisis, do you remember that God is an ever-ready help in time of need? Do you have only a little bit and need a whole lot?

When they saw Jesus, they were troubled, saying, "It's a ghost," and they cried out for fear. When you are facing something difficult and you are troubled, be careful what you say. Fear will always present itself when you are troubled. It will always try to force you into doubt and unbelief. They were tired and worried because of the continuing storm they were battling. Have you ever felt like this? When is Jesus going to show up? Does he know what is going on?

Remember Jesus was upon a mountain praying. When you are praying, storms don't affect you the way they would affect you if you weren't praying.

It is okay to cry out when you are troubled (to be concerned or worried emotionally or mentally disturbed). The disciples cried out for fear. They were feeling hopeless, and to top it all off, a ghost was coming toward them!

Jesus spoke immediately to *them* and not to the crisis (verse 27). He is interested in *how you* handle things rather than how *things are handling you*. God's desire is for you to be more than a conqueror in every situation that rises against you. Jesus will always be there for you.

The first thing that needs to leave during a crisis is fear of failure because fear paralyzes faith. Once that is removed, nothing will be present to hinder your faith.

As soon as Peter spoke directly to Jesus and asked him to prove who he was, Jesus spoke to Peter. "Do not be afraid." Fear is the enemy of faith, and fear will prevent you from moving into your destiny.

In Luke 5, Peter had heard Jesus's same words, "Do not be afraid." Jesus had told Peter to launch out into the deep and let down his nets for a catch. Peter obeyed and reaped two boatloads of fish to the extent the boats began to sink. When he saw the catch, he fell down at Jesus's knees and said, "Depart from me, for I am a sinful man, O Lord." And Jesus said to Peter, "Do not be afraid."

So Peter had heard those words before. It would seem that Peter had an issue with fear and doubt. But after Jesus's death, it seems that he had more faith and courage than all the other disciples. Did you notice on two different occasions that Peter had an encounter involving two things. Two boatloads of fish and the other was when he only had two fish to feed the multitude. The number two represents agreement and union. On both occasions, Peter had to come into agreement with God's word (Jesus is the living word) in order to achieve success.

Has God been made to remind you, "Do not be afraid"? What he has done for you before he will do again if need be. He is not a one-time God. He will come to your aid over and over and over.

Peter said, "Lord, if it is you, command me to come to you on the water."

Peter knew that Jesus would always tell him to do something impossible to his natural thinking. This was Peter's experience with Jesus.

Jesus said one word, "Come."

Jesus said, "*Come* unto me all you who are heavy laden and I will give you rest." It's not a trick. It is an invitation (Matt. 11:28).

He told Peter to come to him…

Peter had good intentions, for he was well on his way but suddenly lost sight of faith in Jesus's words. He started out in faith but just couldn't finish in faith. He was almost there.

Just like the boats began to sink, Peter began to sink. He knew the wind was boisterous when he got out of the boat. They were fighting the wind when Jesus showed up.

But in the midst of a storm, you can experience peace.

I believe when Peter heard Jesus's words, a peace fell upon him that surpassed all understanding…peace that rendered a miracle.

During the time Peter stepped on the water by faith to reach his destiny, something happened that moved him off-track. He didn't stay focused on the Word.

Could Peter have conceded to a "match game"? This intriguing account of Peter's faith and near-death experience is a prime example of Father God's love, concern, and advice for our well-being. He wants our *undivided* attention. As a parent, I loved to teach our children about particular things. I required their undivided attention so that they would genuinely benefit from the advice.

One moment we can be swinging from the chandelier, and the next moment we can be down in the dumps. One moment we can be walking on the water, and the next moment we can be sinking. One moment we can be serving God, and the next moment spread gossip and leave the church.

I have witnessed over the past thirty-eight years at my church that the most spiritual-acting people have turned out to be the flakiest people I have ever seen.

It requires your focus to remain on Jesus. It requires your focus to remain on his words, his commands, and knowing that you can do all things through Christ, who strengthens you.

But thank God, Peter recognized his inability and weakness and cried out *this time in faith*, even though he was afraid, "Lord, save me." What a short prayer!

Notice he didn't call the prayer team or turn in a prayer request for what he needed. Peter prayed a short and sincere prayer. It doesn't take a long prayer to capture God's attention as long as it is from your heart. And I believe Peter was calling to Jesus with all the faith he had. And it was enough.

God expects us to use all of the faith we have, and then he will be faithful to perform what we cannot do ourselves.

Sometimes, we don't think God will hear our prayer. But God will hear and answer any prayer that is according to his will and spoken from the heart. First John 5:14–15 says, "God, I am afraid (be honest) but I believe you can help me."

Peter was experiencing a life-and-death situation, and without Jesus, he was going under.

No one can feel what you are experiencing in the same way you are. Someone may flow with empathy and desire to help, but they would be unable to pray as emotionally intensive about the situation as you would be capable of. That is why it is important that you develop a *personal* faith in Jesus and his desire to help in time of need.

So Peter did cry out in faith because Jesus said, "Oh, you of little faith, why did you doubt" (verse 31)? Why didn't you go all the way? In other words, why did you stop believing?

When doubt gets in, faith leaves.

Jesus associates little faith with doubt. Oh, you of little faith, why did you doubt or have fear?

Anytime you allow doubt to enter and remove your focus from what God has said for you to do or what God has said that you can do, you, in God's mind, have little faith. You will be able to do little. Peter went a little way, but God wants us to go all the way and receive the blessings he has for us. God has a promise and a plan for our lives. Don't stop short of reaching your destiny.

The enemy will always try to bring doubt and fear into anything God has told you to do. Satan will try to create heavy circumstances that compete for your attention.

But cry out in faith to God every time, and he will immediately stretch out his hand and catch you too. Together Peter and Jesus walked safely back to the boat. Jesus will get you back on track, the storm will cease, and you will cross over.

It Is Time to Wait upon the Lord

But they that wait upon the Lord shall renew their strength. (Isa. 40:31, KJV)

To wait on the Lord is to seek out and give undivided attention to what he wants *for* us or what he wants to accomplish *through* us and then *receive* it or *do* it. It is the same as being a server in a restaurant, waiting and watching for the expectations of the guest so that you can comply with their wishes or demands.

The word *wait* means "to look for," "to look eagerly for," and it means to "lie in wait for" (Brown-Driver-Briggs Hebrew Lexicon).

If you are waiting on the Lord, imagine yourself as though you are watching (like a lion for its prey) for someone and preparing to attack. Don't be afraid of the word *attack* because in this case it is a good thing to do!

The word *attack* comes from the original Italian word meaning "to join battle," and it means "to begin to deal with a problem or task in a determined way" (Oxford University Press Dictionary).

So while we watch or wait on Jesus, his presence will come. We then join him in the battle for our mind which can sometimes be a lengthy and difficult struggle. God may reveal strongholds or mind-sets that have taken years to form that will have to be brought into captivity to the obedience of Christ (2 Cor. 10:5).

We "join" him in battle; he reveals to us a problem in our life that is hindering his flow through us. Perhaps he reveals to us something in our life that is an unnecessary weight that's becoming detrimental to our spiritual growth. We do our part by opening our heart to the Holy Spirit and submitting our will to his. We have now joined him in the battle of our mind. For lack of their perseverance with God I have known those who have battled for years to become free of mental strongholds.

It's a sad thing, but people can have extremely sensitive issues that need to be addressed. Maybe they were abused as a child, maybe they have been through several divorces, or maybe they have been involved in adultery or some other form of lust. Any number of issues can present themselves requiring Jesus's help in resolving. Sometimes, it is a lengthy and difficult struggle to overcome some of the pain that we have suffered or experienced. We can, though, always have hope and assurance by *pressing in* Jesus's healing presence will come. By surrendering our heart to him and practicing our newly found freedom in Christ, we have become the owner of a renewed mind! When your mind becomes renewed to the word of God, peace will flood your soul, your mind, your will, and your emotions.

As you enter into the presence of God, be determined to open your heart and turn *off* your mind. You must refuse the thoughts that interfere with your focus on Jesus. It may require some time, but you will get the victory. The more often you soak and wait, the sooner the victory comes. The more often you soak and wait, the deeper you will be in God. The more often you soak and wait, the more you will become *as he is.*

Matthew 11:12 says, "The violent take it by force" (KJV). The word *violent* is taken from a root word meaning "to crowd oneself into or passively to be seized or to take eager advantage of" (Strong's Greek Definition), and the meaning of the word *force,* according to *Oxford University Press,* is "achieve or bring about by effort," and it means "mental or moral strength."

We can rightly assume then that to lie in wait means those who crowd themselves into be seized or take eagerly advantage of shall renew their strength.

We achieve this through *effort* on our part.

What are you wanting to achieve? Are you giving any effort to achieve a greater depth of God's presence?

Blind Bartimaeus

Now they came to Jericho. As he went out of Jericho with his disciples and a great multitude, blind Bartimaeus, the son of Timaeus, sat by the road begging. And when he heard that it was Jesus of Nazareth, he began to cry out and say, "Jesus, Son of David, have mercy on me!"

Then many warned him to be quiet; but he cried out all the more, "Son of David, have mercy on me!"

So Jesus stood still and commanded him to be called. Then they called the blind man, saying to him, "Be of good cheer. Rise, he is calling you."

And throwing aside his garment, he rose and came to Jesus.

So Jesus answered and said to him, "What do you want Me to do for you?"

The blind man said to him, "Rabboni, that I may receive my sight."

Then Jesus said to him, "Go your way; your faith has made you well."

And immediately he received his sight and followed Jesus on the road. (Mark 10:46–52, NKJV)

When you begin to reach out to the Lord, know that you will have to face some degree of opposition.

The Bible holds the record of a blind man, a beggar whose name was Bartimaeus. Jesus and his disciples were leaving Jericho, along with a great multitude of people. Bartimaeus heard that Jesus was passing by, so he unashamedly cried out to Jesus. By this blatant cry for help, Bartimaeus was near the beginning of a miracle. Why? Because he became of good courage and seized the moment. He knew who Jesus *was*, the promised seed of Abraham—the seed that would come to bring sight to the blind, open deaf ears, deliver those in bondage, heal the brokenhearted, and set free the captives. He believed *in the promise*. Many people rebuked him and told him to be quiet. When you are convinced of a *truth*, no one can convince you otherwise; no one can keep you quiet.

Do not allow the enemy of your faith to rob your peace and joy. Do not allow fear to rob you of a miracle.

Prior to Jesus's presence, Bartimaeus had no joy. He had nothing to look forward to each day, only to wake up and routinely beg for help. Realizing that he might not have another chance for a visitation of God, Bartimaeus cried out to Jesus even *louder* asking for mercy. It took great courage and desperation for a blind man to cause such a commotion, because he was considered an outcast.

What the enemy intends for harm, God will turn it around for your good. If Bartimaeus had listened to the people and lost courage, he would not have captured Jesus's attention. If Bartimaeus had been consumed with the fact that he was blind, poor, and helpless, he would have been focused on his problems and not on Jesus, the answer. If Bartimaeus had been murmuring and complaining about his hardships, he would not have heard that Jesus was near. If he had been gossiping or complaining to another beggar about how unfair life had been to him, he would have missed his miracle. He would have been murmuring instead of listening. But he *was* listening! Although he was sitting beside a multitude, this blind man had trained his ears to hear *beyond* the noisy world around him. We must train our *spiritual* ears to hear what the Holy Spirit is saying *inside* us. It's possible to train yourself to recognize in the natural realm as well, the different ways in which he communicates to us.

I have recognized God's communication through unusual occurrences, sounds at odd times, finding feathers at unusual or random places in my home, someone calling me at the same time I am calling them, same repeated circumstances occurring, etc.

How many times has Jesus been near and you weren't *watching or hearing*? How many miracles have passed by you unaware?

When Bartimaeus *cried out even louder* was the moment Jesus took notice. God is drawn to brokenhearted people. I believe Jesus was not only drawn to the faith of this blind man, but he was drawn to the injustice and apathy that was taking place. It took faith for Bartimaeus to ignore the opposition of the people because no one had respect for him. Bartimaeus could have easily given up, but he resisted the temptation and continued in faith, and Jesus stopped for him. (God always honors faith.) Jesus then called for *him*. Do you know if Jesus has called for you?

Do you know that Jesus will hear you too? You may be feeling weary in your mind. You may feel like giving up. You might be tired of depending on other people, depending on their faith to get your prayers answered. You may think that God does not hear your prayers. You may be hearing doubt from the enemy. Don't give up! Keep reaching out to God in faith, and he will help you. Stay focused on God! Draw near to God, and he will draw near to you (James 4:8, NET). It could be that God has already shown a way or spoken an answer, but you've been too busy to be still (and quiet) before him and *know* that he is God.

Bartimaeus's faith is the very thing that got Jesus's attention. He could have given up; after all, he was a blind beggar. It didn't get much worse than that in the eyes of the public (unless you were a leper). You may feel you are at the bottom of the barrel, so to speak. You may feel that no one loves or cares about you. You may feel you have nothing to offer anyone. Maybe you need mercy.

Jesus called for Bartimaeus to come to *him*. Jesus requires you to come face-to-face with him, a place of intimacy. Through faith, Bartimaeus threw off his cloak, his stigma, knowing he would no longer be a blind beggar, for he was ready to receive his miracle! He was ready to become useable and profitable in society. He was about to have a purpose in life. He was about to receive a new lifestyle. The Bible doesn't mention anyone leading him to Jesus; Bartimaeus simply followed the sound of his voice. Notice when he came face-to-face with Jesus, he asked Bartimaeus what he wanted him to do for him.

What do you want Jesus to do for you? Do you need a healing? Do you need a financial miracle? Are you tired of your lifestyle and want one that glorifies God? Do you want deliverance? Come face-to-face with Jesus, and tell him what you *want*.

Know this, need and desire are two different things. God said to come *boldly* to his throne to receive *mercy* and *find* grace. The blind man needed eyesight, but more importantly, he *wanted* it. When you *want* something that much, you will burst the "sound barrier of faith" to be heard. He was tired of his lifestyle as a beggar. He was tired of begging for food every day. He was "fed up" with people talking down to him. He was tired of missing out on life. He wanted to contribute to his community rather than be a drain to it.

Bartimaeus came right to the point, "I want to see!" He didn't say to Jesus, "I don't deserve it, but would you heal my eyes?" He came in faith that Jesus, the teacher, was not a respecter of persons. He evidently had heard of Jesus and had faith because Bartimaeus called Jesus Rabboni. Our faith comes from hearing the word of God (Rom. 10:17). Either you believe the Word (Jesus was and is the living Word), or you don't. Bartimaeus believed.

It's that simple with God. You must show God your faith by your works, your works of faith! God wants us to come boldly to his throne of grace to obtain what *we* need. You cannot come boldly unless you believe you are going to leave *with* what you came for.

Bartimaeus simply said to Jesus that he wanted to receive his sight.

Have you lost sight of your faith? Have you lost sight of your vision? Have you allowed circumstances to overcome your confidence in God? You may need to receive new sight and regain the focus you once had in the things of God. Maybe you can't see as clearly as you once could and your faith is wavering. Maybe you need to have your vision strengthened.

There is, however, some action required on your part. It is not all God, and it is not all you. It is God *and* you, God in you achieving the goal of renewed strength. Without faith, no one can please God (Heb. 11:6). Do you think that you can receive anything from God without "pleasing faith"? Do you have faith that he is going to reward you when you diligently seek him (Heb. 11:6)? It is God doing his part and you doing yours. He has already provided everything we will ever need, and our part is to *take* what we need by *faith*.

They who make waiting on Jesus their focus will renew their strength and power and become in closer relationship to God. It's interesting to note that one of the definitions of the word *focus* is to "adapt to the prevailing level of light and become able to see clearly" (Oxford University Press Dictionary). For example, if you were to get up in the middle of the night, the lights in your house would not be on. You would have to wait for a few seconds so that your eyes could become adjusted to the level or degree of light in your house. Even though the electricity is not on, some trace or level of light would be in your house, whether it was from the moon shining through your window or maybe from a floodlight outside. Nevertheless, some level of light would be in the room, and you would have to wait until your eyes became focused so that you could see clearly enough to move without stumbling.

Jesus said in John 9:5, "As long as I am in the world I am the light of the world" (NKJV).

Now *we* are the light of the world because Jesus, by the Holy Spirit, lives in us.

So we must remain focused on Jesus, the light in us, and adapt to the direction given by the Holy Spirit. By doing so, our light level will not only enable *us* to see clearly what God wants and desires from us, but it will shine to others who need Jesus. They will see that light in us.

As we wait on the Lord to renew our strength, we are allowing the Lord to give fresh strength to us. When our strength becomes freshened, the living water in us becomes fit to give to others to drink.

By waiting on the Lord, you will be able to "resume or reestablish after an interruption" (Oxford University Press Dictionary).

We all have experienced interruptions in our lives.

Your life may have been interrupted because of a divorce. Maybe you are suffering heartache from the death of a loved one. Maybe your car was repossessed. There are all kinds of interruptions in our lives. "Many are the afflictions of the righteous, but the Lord delivers him out of them all" (Ps. 34:19, NKJV).

Maybe you have been diagnosed with a terminal disease.

What are you going to do when your life is interrupted? You must be able to adapt to the prevailing level of light so that you can see what to do. At what level is the light in you? (As we walk with God in *his* righteousness, our pathway grows brighter and brighter.) Walking with the Lord is always going to be a *faith* walk. Believing, trusting, and faith will always be necessary components.

This is how the level of light increases: (1) draw near and have Jesus as your focus; (2) lie in wait; (3) expect and look eagerly for Jesus (you will need faith that Jesus is going to show up and help) and when he does; (4) attack the problem with him, and work *with* him by opening your heart and surrendering your all to him; (5) read the written Word of God, and ask him to give you understanding of it; (6) pray every day as often as possible; and (7) don't just hear or read the word but practice it.

That is your part—surrendering and obeying. Admit to him that he is God and without him you can do nothing to bring about effectual change in your life. Approach God with a humble heart. At some point, you are required to step out in faith and do what you feel God (the Holy Spirit) is saying. This is also *your* part in reaching your destiny.

I don't know any example in the Word of God of anyone crying out to the Lord and the Lord not hearing and coming to their rescue. Israel cried out to the Lord for over four hundred years while they were in slavery to Egypt. God not only delivered them out of their misery but showered them with great possessions as they left Egypt. He heard them, and he hears you. Isn't it a comfort knowing that it won't take four hundred years for *your* miracle or deliverance to happen?

Hosea 6:3 reads, "Then shall we know if we follow on to know the Lord: his going forth is prepared as the morning; and he shall come unto us as the rain, as the latter and former rain of the earth" (KJV).

God is always near us. Therefore, he is always near when we are in trouble. He goes before us and makes the crooked ways straight (Isa. 42:16, NKJV).

Jesus said he would lead us beside the waters that are calm and give renewed strength and energy to our souls (Ps. 23). That is the path on which the *Lord* leads us, but sometimes, *we* take the lead unaware. When that happens, the electrical in our navigation system "short-circuits," bringing a delay to our purpose.

By our own effort, we will fall into a place of unrest, and that undertow will take you where God never intended for you to go. But God, in his mercy, will hear your cry for help and send angels to minister for you. God may, however, allow you to remain for a while in that place of unsettlement. His motive being that you will learn again to trust him. That is how you grow and mature in God.

God uses your mistakes to reveal *his* goodness and *your* character. We can fall victim to a lot of trouble and needless heartaches. Our souls can be so full of pain because of the trials and pressures that come upon us. But through them all, we can trust our daddy God to lead us back in the pathway to victory. Hopefully, by the time we reach victory, we will have learned a valuable lesson. Hopefully, we will have matured in that particular area of our life and will know how to avoid future pitfalls.

When we wait on the Lord and when we drink the living water that Jesus speaks of, we become refreshed. Because his Spirit is so satisfying, our emotional needs and desires become complete. Our strength is renewed. Our hope is stirred again that everything is going to be okay.

As we wait in God's presence, as we listen to worship music, our faith is strengthened, our minds become rested, and peace fills our souls. Peace fills our mind, will, and emotions. We may enter God's presence feeling one way, but we will leave feeling differently. Why? Because the Holy Spirit has poured out upon us. He pours out strength, comfort, peace, and joy. He speaks to our hearts and gives direction or sometimes gives warning that we are about to make a mistake. He might whisper, "Don't take that job," "Don't marry that man," "Don't marry that woman," etc., because God knows everything about your future and he desires it to be good. He will always give something better to you than you had. He desires for you to prosper in every area of your life. You will prosper and be in good health *as your soul* prospers (3 John 1:2). What are you waiting for?

God may tell you to continue in the direction in which you are headed. That would be some reassuring news, wouldn't it?

Jeremiah 29:11 says, "For I know the thoughts that I think toward you, says the Lord, thoughts of peace and not evil, to give you a future and a hope" (NKJV).

Psalm 139:17 says, "How precious also are Your thoughts to me, O God! How great is the sum of them! If I should count them, they would be more in number than the sand" (NKJV).

That tells me that I am always on God's mind and that he is continually aware of my comings and goings. But is *my* mind upon God, looking unto him to direct my comings and goings so that I won't wind up in the wrong place at the wrong time?

We wait on the Lord, and courage rises within our hearts. Fear leaves. Depression leaves. Hearts are changed. Love is restored.

Psalm 27:14 says that David said, "The Lord is my light and my salvation: Whom shall I fear? Wait on the Lord; be of good courage and he shall strengthen your heart; Wait, I say, on the Lord" (NKJV)!

Courage will give strength to face life's pain and grief. God has purpose for your life, but you are the one who must get tuned in; you must adjust yourself to his frequency so that you can clearly hear his voice.

John 10:4–5 says, "When he has brought his own sheep outside he walks on before them, and his sheep follow him because they know his voice. They will never [on any account] follow a stranger, but will run away from him because they do not know the voice of strangers or recognize their call" (AMP).

We are not only called out of the world, but it is vital that we continue in Christ and the faith to which we are called.

Jesus said that he is the door and any who enters shall live and go in and out and find pasture (John 10:9). In Jesus, you can find spiritual food to eat for growth and increase because he is the Bread of Life (John 6:48). "We are, like newborn babies [*thirst for, crave, earnestly desire*] the sincere, the pure spiritual milk of the word that by it we may be nurtured and grow unto [completed] salvation" (AMP).

First Peter 2:2 (AMP) says we are to partake of the law of faith so we might grow up and so that we might increase in the things of God. When we increase in the things of God, he causes every good thing in our life to increase. We must decrease in order for him to increase in us (John 3:30). We have to allow him room in our heart to make adjustments.

We are to provide lodging or sufficient space for the work of the Holy Spirit and adapt to or fit in with what he desires to accomplish in us.

Third John 1:2 says, "Beloved, I pray that you may prosper in all things and be in health, just as your soul prospers…just as you walk in the truth" (NKJV). That was worth repeating!

God loves us. Period. He has provided all of the necessary or appropriate parts for the body of Christ to be entire and complete. He wants us to be fully satisfied in him. He wants us to finish our course and tell others who don't know him to do the same thing. Jesus went out of *his* way for us. He laid down his life for us. That is saying it mildly. It is time we went out of *our* way for him. It is time we laid down our premature agendas for him and say, "Lord, not my will but your will be done."

As we wait on the Lord, we are waiting for him to lead us. We are not as sheep who are to wander away, "doing our own thing." If we wait on him and grasp that which he supplies, we will find that we will be in green pastures. He has promised to bring us to a place of peace and prosperity, and as we are resting there, we will find restoration for our souls; in other words, we will be made to rest in a pleasant place.

In the Song of Solomon 5:16, we have a picture of the Bride of Christ speaking about her beloved. She says, "His voice and speech are exceedingly sweet; yes he is altogether lovely [the whole of him delights and is precious]. This is my beloved, and this is my friend, O daughters of Jerusalem" (AMP).

The more often we wait on the Lord and the more often we seek his lovely face, the greater he becomes altogether lovely to us. We are able to see him more clearly. We become complete in him and experience that he *is* a pleasant habitation, a place to hide.

CPSIA information can be obtained
at www.ICGtesting.com
Printed in the USA
LVHW031934111119
637013LV00020B/838/P